FEASTING ON GOD'S WORD

From frozen food to gourmet banquet

DAVID SPRIGGS

This book is gratefully dedicated to all who have helped me to enjoy the Bible—from Sunday school teachers at the Hoby Methodist chapel, to scholars like Eichrodt and von Rad; from parents and friends who lived its truth, to my family who encourage me to try; from creative people who stimulate my imagination, to prayerful people who energize my work. Above all, my thanks to God and all whose toil through the centuries gives me the opportunity to 'search the scriptures' today.

CONTENTS

Introduction: Why and how this book works............................6

1 Play it..11

2 Re-write it 30

3 Display it 42

4 Eat it..56

5 Twist it...73

6 Pray it 92

7 Study it..108

8 Do it...123

9 Give it away...141

Conclusion 153

Resources 154

INTRODUCTION

4 July 2000 was a special day, not only for the USA (as it is every year) but for the Bible. It was the day chosen for the launch of the first reprint of the Tyndale New Testament in the original spelling. The launch took place at the prestigious British Library in London. In the 16th century, William Tyndale's translation was paid for at the cost of his own life, but his influence on Britain and the English language is incalculable. Many of our favourite phrases, such as 'fight the good fight' and 'the powers that be', are his gift to us. His desire was that the 'boy who drives the plough' would have access to the Bible and knowledge of it. And for centuries his translation into comfortable English succeeded.

While I was attending the launch, I had the opportunity to speak to one of the executives from Wycliffe Bible Translators. John Wycliffe, after whom that organization is named, inspired an earlier epoch-making translation into contemporary English, so it is appropriate that 'Wycliffe' should be devoted to translating the scriptures. I was informed that they have celebrated their 500th translation of the New Testament recently and this amazing feat has been accomplished in around 50 years. Try to imagine that! The Bible is unquestionably the most influential book in the English language and the most translated book in the world. That is not primarily a testimony to the imperialistic success of the nations that have nurtured the Bible and its translation, such as Germany, Spain and England, but more a testimony to the universal appeal and significance of the Bible itself.

So what has gone wrong at home? Not only are there fewer and fewer people going to church but there are fewer people reading the Bible both within the Christian community and in wider society. Inevitably this means a decrease in knowledge of what is in the Bible, its stories, its wisdom, its directives, its central character—God. It also means a decrease in its transformational impact on people and culture. The Bible has immeasurably enriched us and is a massive asset—but that asset has become 'frozen'—no longer available for us to draw on. We can speculate for a long time as to why this is happening, and I am fortunate to work for an organization that is committed to reversing this trend.

I am not simplistic enough to think that this book can reverse the trend on its own, but it is written out of a broad awareness and a deep sorrow that the Bible is a neglected treasure and one that we neglect at our peril. So the book's intention is to encourage us to experience the power of the Bible in new ways. Hence the subtitle, 'From frozen food to gourmet banquet'. When I go round the frozen food counters in the supermarket, I am stimulated! Everything is in such colourful and enticing packaging, from pizzas to profiteroles, from seafood to pavlovas, from fish in batter to beefburgers. All this food offers the potential for producing gourmet meals, but only once someone has done some creative work with it. Try eating it straight out of the freezer! It needs people to prepare it and, to be truly worthwhile, it warrants a suitable occasion—such as a party or a celebration complete with a crowd of people ready to make the most of it. As I look at the Bible, it reminds me of those frozen food counters—I know the attractive packaging and the potential of the contents. But regrettably many people are in too much of a hurry to browse. Rushing through their routine shopping list, they do not even see the attractive packaging, let alone experience in their imaginations the stimulation of creating fabulous food for great occasions. So, in relation to the Bible, this book aims to entice people to look inside the packaging and prepare and enjoy some meals.

One of the Bible's favourite self-descriptions is food. For instance, Jesus in his well-known rebuff to Satan says, 'Human beings cannot live on bread alone, but need every word that God speaks' (Matthew 4:4, quoting Deuteronomy 8:3). So it is entirely appropriate to use this kind of metaphor. The Bible sees itself as absolutely essential for life— bread, but more necessary than physical bread. But it also sees itself, as we would say, as 'the icing on the cake'—as honey dripping enticingly from the honeycomb.

Personally, I enjoy studying the Bible, with the help of commentaries and Bible encyclopedias. Spending hours on Bible word studies is, for me, great fun. I even enjoy preparing and preaching sermons. After forty years of intensive study I still find the Bible amazingly fresh and challenging. However, I also understand that my ways are probably not your ways and I have discovered many other more creative ways to engage with the Bible. So this book suggests a variety of different ways in which you might enjoy the Bible. That is one of its first aims. I have collected together a number of different approaches, some of which will work for you, others maybe not—but at least give them all a try. I believe that when we start to look at the Bible as a source of rich enjoyment, even fun, God will find it easier to speak to us through it, because we shall come to it with anticipation and enthusiasm.

In order to help this, the emphasis is on active involvement with scripture. We have begun to move away from thinking that only the preacher has anything useful to contribute about the Bible. For the last 25 years there has been a growth in home-based study groups and other small groups, and in the materials to service them. Often, however, the range of approaches used in such groups is rather limited and they can eventually become a few people sitting rather comfortably, only just above the snooze level of consciousness. The Bible then ceases to stir and stimulate. Soon—surprise, surprise—people become rather bored with the Bible. Indeed, I have noticed that it is often while the coffee is being prepared that the most engaging conversations of the evening take place. So this book works on the principle that if we become more active in our approaches to the Bible, we might find it has more to offer us. Admiring the garden from a sunny seat has its place, but real fun usually involves some action, whether working on or playing in the garden. And the more work you put into the garden the more rewarding it is to gaze at.

Each of the main chapters follows a similar pattern, as follows:

- **Ice-breakers**: these are enjoyable exercises for people in groups to help them develop their relationships and, if they are new to the group, to settle down. They do not normally involve any biblical knowledge or engagement with the Bible; they relate to our ordinary experiences. In this book there is a connection with the theme of the chapter too—so they help to tune people into the subject or the approach to be followed.

- **Introduction:** this sets the scene; it explains the scope and some-times the relevance of the approach dealt with in the chapter.
- **Bible study:** this seeks to engage people with the subject of the chapter by linking directly to appropriate material in the Bible; it does this often in novel ways.
- **Practical ideas:** here you will discover a range of activities which enable you to explore practically the issues being considered.
- **Further afield:** this section suggests one or more ways in which people can develop their understanding by visiting a place where they can make further discoveries.
- **Prayer:** the chapter concludes with a brief prayer which relates to the topic of the chapter. Groups may wish to end their evening with this prayer each time they meet. Alternatively they may wish to develop their own prayers.

There is one final thing to note about the way this book is planned. Essentially, you can start at any chapter which appeals to you and it will take you to the same place as any other chapter—an appetizing encounter with scripture.

So, each chapter is seeking to show, first, that the Bible can be an enjoyable book; second, that the Bible is a stimulant for activity; and third, that the Bible invites us to be discoverers of its truths and values for ourselves and not simply sponges to soak up other people's views about it. Finally and most importantly (but also most scarily), we should remember that through active engagement with the Bible we may meet God in fresh ways too.

GETTING GOING

There are all kinds of ways to use this book, either on your own or in a group, although I would suggest that whenever possible you involve a group, as it is likely to be more fun and more enriching. Here are three main ways to use the material.

- Use the 'ice-breakers', one or two at a time, for the start of your normal home group meetings.
- Use some of the Bible studies found normally towards the start of each chapter.
- Take a chapter each week and try out some of the activities. Perhaps you could have a ten-session course to cover all the topics. If your church has a number of home groups, why not try different activities within any topic and then share your experiences?

At the end of the book there is a Resources section (p. 154). This has some general contact information, followed by specific resources for each chapter. Please remember that this section is there to help you.

Finally for now, although I have used a variety of translations of the Bible, my standard one is the Good News Bible, so if you are not told otherwise, that is where any quotation will come from.

PRAYER

Perhaps this seems to you like the challenge of climbing a mountain! So why not imagine that you are looking at a mountain—like Snowdon— and wondering whether to climb it or not. It is enticing in its beauty, but its terrain and the distance to the summit are daunting. How would you encourage yourself to make a start? Are you with friends who are good company? Will you think of the views and the beauty you will miss if you don't go? Will it be helpful to think that you can take your time and rest along the way? Perhaps you have always wanted to tackle this challenge and now is your chance. Maybe what will get you going is anticipating the sense of achievement when you are standing on the summit.

Father God, as we start our journey through this book, help us not to be afraid either of the challenges it will bring, or of the fear of failure if we do not complete our tasks. Rather, encourage us through your Holy Spirit to make a start, trusting that however short or long our exploration, we will have gained much both for ourselves and to share with others. We ask this through Jesus Christ our Lord. Amen.

Chapter 1

PLAY IT

ICE-BREAKERS

1. Think back to your childhood. What was your favourite toy—a doll, teddy bear, electric train, Meccano set or other construction toy? Spend a couple of minutes enjoying some memories of it. What feeling does it evoke? What did it look like, feel like? Can you recall some especially happy moments with your toy? And were there any sad or painful experiences associated with this toy—when you lost your favourite teddy, for instance, or when your brother mocked your construction?

   What are your feelings towards that toy now? Do you still possess it or have you bought a similar one for your children, grandchildren or even yourself?

   Did you learn any particular skills or lessons through that toy? If you enjoyed looking after a 'sick doll', did you end up as a nurse? If a racing car was your favourite, have you become a speedy driver?

   After a few minutes, join up in threes and share your memories and experiences.

   Can you see connections between other people's favourite toys and who they are and what they do now?

2. What is your favourite team game, or do you hate them? Compile a list of everybody's preferences. Invite someone who is passionate

11

about a particular sport to explain (a) the rules and how they operate; and (b) why the game is so good and enjoyable. Are you any the wiser?

Are team games important? What is especially enjoyable about them? If you don't like them, do you know why?

3. Invite everyone to bring a musical instrument—provide percussion ones and 'tin whistles' for those who come without one (perhaps you could borrow these from your church's children's workers, or from a local school). As a group, you have to (a) decide which hymn or song you will perform and sing to celebrate God's goodness; and (b) perform it.

Please remember that God loves a joyful performer as well as a cheerful giver (see 2 Corinthians 9:7). He values us giving all we have, even if it's only a little, rather than being brilliant and not offering it all! (see Luke 21:2–4).

INTRODUCTION

Play is serious business. Today vast resources are ploughed into toy manufacture and vast profits made. But the resources are more than financial: they are creative and imaginative, and the investment includes skilful manufacture and marketing as well as money. Toys need to be researched and tested very thoroughly. To produce new toys is a demanding but fruitful aspect of human enterprise.

It is also true that much creative energy goes into some forms of play, whether it is constructing cars from kits or imagining the conversations between the latest fashion dolls. On top of this there is the educational value of play. If parents do not know how to play with their children, then those children are disadvantaged. Even with adult team training, play is recognized to be a useful element. So when I encourage you to 'play' the Bible, that is not the same thing at all as saying that the Bible is unimportant. Far from it—I believe the Bible is so important that we need to engage with it and encounter it in all sorts of new ways that will stimulate our relationship with it, and challenge us to apply its vision and message in new contexts. Adults, as well as children, learn huge amounts through play. Nevertheless, I have chosen the heading 'Play it' to remind us that it can be fun for us as well.

There are many different connotations to 'play it'. Before we get down to some actions, let's unpack the phrase a bit.

Firstly, there is the sense of to 'play music' and, of course, when people play a piece of music they need an instrument—but we'll come to that in a minute. What happens when someone plays a piece of music is fascinating. With their eyes they read a score on a page—a series of marks, mostly musical notes, which have a certain significance through an agreed convention—and they translate that score into something that other people encounter through their hearing, which may touch their emotions or their intellect; it may stir all kinds of memories or it may motivate them to great heroics or romance. What begins as a personal reading becomes a public event. That is something we need to do with and for the Bible. Many people cannot read the 'notes' of the Bible, just as I cannot read the notes of music, but they can appreciate the sounds it makes, sounds of human longing, divine visitation, the search for meaning, how to live and die well and so on. That, it seems to me, is one of the ways in which presenting the Bible as drama helps people: it enables them to experience a text that they would not otherwise be able to understand and appreciate.

What else does the musical meaning of 'playing' have to show us about the Bible? People who play an instrument need to become very attached to it if they are to get the best from it. Last night I was fortunate enough to be at an orchestral concert where James Galway was both conducting and playing his flute. I noticed how, when he played the flute, it became an extension of who he was. It was as though the gleaming metal was an integral part of his body, completing his physical being and enhancing his powers to communicate. If the Bible, or some part of it, becomes for a time integrated with us, or us with it, then this can be a very moving experience. 'Hot seating' (see later in this chapter) can provide this kind of encounter.

Another meaning of 'play' relates to playing a game. Some games are designed to be educational, and they have their place—we will look at some which help us to enter the world of the Bible. Many games are not designed to be educational, however; they are intended simply for enjoyment. Even so, we can still learn a tremendous amount from them about ourselves, other people or, indeed, how the world in general works. I suspect that one of the reasons why many people have been put off the Bible is because they have perceived it as a rule book for a life of hard work. But actually, if we take a closer look at the Bible we will discover a great deal of playfulness there.

As we turn to our Bible study section, however, we will explore yet another angle on 'play'—as it relates to the world of drama.

BIBLE STUDY

In one sense the whole biblical story is a divine drama, and many would see the climactic scene in the crucifixion. But within every drama there are sub-plots with their highs and lows. One of the great 'dramatic moments' in the Gospel story is Jesus' entry into Jerusalem on Palm Sunday. You will find a version of this in all four Gospels, but we are about to look at Matthew's, which you will find in chapter 21:1–11. So please take time to read that passage now.

There are three reasons why I select this as a dramatic 'high point'. First, there is a lot of action, the scene is extremely colourful and lively, and the setting is cinematic with the view of Jerusalem as Jesus comes over the ridge of the Mount of Olives. It is like a series of concentric circles with Jesus in the middle, then the disciples, next the cheering crowd, all bathed in the glory of the sunlight—but in the shadows is another circle, ominous and sinister, consisting of all who oppose Jesus' reign. In this scene there is a sense of gathering up all that has gone before and, at the same time, a sense that this is the prelude to all that is to come. Beyond the obvious excitement and growing conflict, there is the hint of mystery. Take the arrangement about the donkey, for instance: how did Jesus know it would be available? Had he made secret arrangements with the owner? If so, what else had he 'plotted' in advance? Or was it some kind of prophetic awareness, just as he was aware that he would be arrested and crucified?

Second, at a deeper level, this scene is about Jesus challenging all the powers—the powers of Judaism and the temple hierarchy; indeed ultimately, of course, the whole sacrificial system that his one sacrifice is going to replace. Then he is challenging the power of nationalism, as his 'passive' entrance (on a donkey, not a war horse) depicts so vividly. Then he is challenging the power of Rome, as he has the audacity to enter the city with a kind of 'victory parade', something reserved only for emperors and victorious generals. Finally, he is challenging Satan to release his captives.

Third, there is still another kind of dramatic layer to all this, connecting with biblical liturgy and history. Take the shout of the crowd: 'Praise to David's Son! God bless him who comes in the name of the Lord! Praise God' (Matthew 21:9). This links to the *Hallel* Psalms (so called because they were a special group of psalms of 'praise': think of 'hallelujah'—it means 'praise Yahweh'), particularly Psalm 118:26. These psalms had their own dramatic use in Judaism, as they were part of the processional ritual as people approached Jerusalem, a ritual familiar to all pilgrims. Earlier in Israel's history, they were used in the temple worship.

Psalm 118 tells us a moving story of distress, with a sense of defeat overwhelming the psalmist. It then moves through hints of an amazing divine rescue and on to a call to others to celebrate this victory and a suggestion of their response. The antiphonal response of verses 1–4 shifts to the storytelling of verses 5–14. Then, in verse 19, comes the appeal to be allowed to enter the temple to offer thanksgiving and confirm the victory. This is followed by the challenge from within the temple at verse 20; verse 21 may be the claim to be 'righteous' and so eligible to process into the temple. Verses 22–25 seem to be the verdict on the appeal to 'open the gates'. Verses 26–29 hint at more of this sacred drama, with first the temple staff blessing those who come, followed by their public affirmation of God's goodness, concluding with the temple staff instructing the new arrivals to start the procession.

After exploring the connection with Psalm 118, we can discern a new significance in Matthew's portrayal of Jesus' arrival in Jerusalem. For, like a stage suddenly becoming floodlit, we can discern something new. Hidden in the crowd's words is the demand that the temple should be open to Jesus, and implicit in their marching around Jesus may be the claim that he is to become the altar (see Psalm 118:27)! His entry is the beginning of a new festival.

Here are comedy and tragedy all rolled into one. Here is vivid action undergirded with both sinister and transcendent resonances.

To what extent did your church's Palm Sunday service convey some of this intense drama? What could you do to bring out some of these dramatic qualities in your service next year?

So, let's turn to ways in which we can 'play' with the Bible as our source. Our first exploration looks at some ways in which games can help us engage with the Bible; then we will develop the drama theme in a number of ways.

GAMES

Playing games is an important way to get involved with the Bible in a fun way. You can buy ready-made Bible-based games, and your local Christian bookshop will help you to identify suitable ones. Also, for those who want PC-based games, you can ask for the *Christian Software Catalogue* (free).

It can, however, be more fun and also more informative to construct your own games. Here are a couple of 'home-made' examples to get you started.

WILDERNESS WANDERINGS

You will need:
- A standard Ludo board
- Four counters (or Exodus characters—see later)
- A dice

You will need to make:
- Four sets of six 'pass cards' (each card about 6cm x 5cm, and each set being numbered 1–6). These 'pass cards' need to be labelled as follows:

    Set 1: six of the plagues of Egypt (Exodus 8—11)

    Set 2: the first six commandments (Exodus 20:1–17)

    Set 3: six sites from the wilderness wanderings (for example, Red Sea, the Desert of Sin, Sinai, Rephidim, Meribah, the Plains of Moab

    Set 4: six articles from the Tabernacle (Exodus 25—31)
- Two larger cards (10cm x 7cm), one with 'Wilderness' written on it, the other with 'Promised Land'

Place a set of pass cards on each of the 'home bases' of the Ludo board and put the Promised Land and Wilderness cards in the centre of the board.

The object of the game is to collect one each of the Plagues, Commandments, Sites and Tabernacle pass cards and then to exchange these four cards for the Promised Land card. The first person to do this is the winner—they have made it to the Promised Land. (A reward of 'milk and honey' such as a chocolate bar is permitted!)

To start the game, players can place their counter wherever they choose on the outer perimeter of the board squares, but make sure you note exactly where each player starts (see 'The Wilderness', below).

Players proceed by throwing the dice and moving their counter the appropriate number of squares; if they throw a six they have another throw but move straight to this final position. Players can choose which direction they travel round the board, but that direction remains the same until they have collected a pass card, when they can change direction.

- **'The Wilderness'**: If a player lands on another player, that player is moved on to the Wilderness card in the centre of the board. In order to escape from the Wilderness, players must throw either a six or the number on any of the pass cards they have collected. When they have thrown their 'release number' they return to the main board, taking up their original starting position. They then have a further throw to start them on their journey again.

- **Pass cards:** To collect a pass card, players must reach the 'home base' where the stack is placed. They do not need to throw an exact number to obtain their card. Having obtained the card, they have an additional throw, to restart their wanderings.
- **Character counters:** If you wish, you can choose characters from the Exodus story (for example, Pharaoh, Moses, Aaron, Miriam), write the names on labels and stick them on the counters.

Wilderness Wanderings is a good way of bringing alive the Exodus story. If you involve your group in making the pass cards, they can be encouraged to read the stories in order to make their selection of six commandments (or whatever), even decorating the cards with symbols or pictures to represent the words. And as you play you can pause and think about the events and places mentioned.

The same game structure can be adapted to fit other parts of the Bible. For instance, it can be called 'Disciple', where the journey is following Jesus through his ministry, and the pass cards feature Beatitudes, parables, miracles and words from the cross. The Wilderness can become Herod's Fortress and the Promised Land becomes the Empty Tomb.

BIBLICAL SCRABBLE

You will need a standard Scrabble set.

Play according to the standard rules of Scrabble, apart from one crucial factor: any word of four or more letters must relate to:

- a book of the Bible, for example, Ruth, Luke or Acts or even Leviticus
- a biblical character such as David, Paul or Mary
- a biblical theme, such as creation, mission, parents or wisdom.

Obviously you will need to drop the normal Scrabble ban on proper names.

In the case of biblical themes, if the other players dispute the legitimacy of a particular word, then the player concerned needs to present their case, with the others taking a decision. This will build awareness and understanding of the biblical text (as well as the practices of listening and forgiving!).

The benefit of the game is clear: as they play, people's minds will be hard at work scanning and revisiting their biblical knowledge. While the game depends on people's knowledge, it also promotes ingenuity, particularly with the thematic version.

DRAMA

There are many different ways in which the Bible and drama can be effective partners. We can use role-play, write our own drama or even ad-lib a well-known biblical story. Of course, many films, musicals, poems and plays have been developed from the Bible's sub-plots.

DRAMATIC MOMENTS

Ask each person in the group to make a list of their five 'most dramatic moments' in the Bible. The expulsion of Adam and Eve from the Garden of Eden appealed to the poet Milton; Joseph and his amazing coloured coat entranced Andrew Lloyd Webber and Tim Rice; Handel wrote an oratorio around the great events in Elijah's life. But who or what stirs your memories?

Having made your lists and talked about them together (if you are short on time, then take each person's first two choices and go round again as time permits), try to work out what it is about each incident that makes it so memorable. Some of the issues you may wish to look out for are tragedy/comedy, adventure/mystery, violence/intrigue, power/sex, love/revenge, strong/appealing characters—but of course, please expect other things to be noted too.

IMPACT DRAMA

One kind of Bible drama is re-enacting a familiar Bible story. Normally this is to bring out a specific point or to focus on a specific issue. Examples are readily available, such as Tim Storey's *Conversations on the Way* (Kevin Mayhew, 2001), and David Burt's *50 Sketches about Jesus* (Kingsway, 1999) or *25 Sketches about Proverbs* (Kingsway, 2000). You could also look out for second-hand copies of *Cracking the Church Cocoon* by Mandy Watsham and Nicki Matthews' (BRF, out of print).

It is important to realize that such dramatic representations can have a wide range of effects. The most obvious moment of impact is when the play is performed. But the drama also impacts those who learn the parts and live through the characters. The re-living of the performance through the memories of all who took part or watched must be noted too. One effect that we can most easily overlook involves those who write the scripts we use. We will start here.

Obviously the first step in 'playing' the Bible by re-enactment is to select a passage and read it aloud. Make your choice, allocate parts to different people and have a go. Some of the factors that may affect your choice are the season in the Christian year when you plan to perform, or the subject you wish to explore, but make sure that your passage has dramatic qualities and that it appeals to you all. It is often helpful to have a 'narrator', but allocate as much of the story as possible to individual characters, even if the actual words of the Bible passage are about them rather than spoken by them. Passages you could use include Jesus' entry into Jerusalem, which we referred to earlier, or Moses and Aaron confronting Pharaoh (either Exodus 5:1–20 or 7:1–13), Hannah's experience in the temple (1 Samuel 1:9–20), David's compassion towards Mephibosheth (2 Samuel 9:1–13), Paul and Barnabas at Lystra (Acts 14:6–18) or Paul's experiences in Malta (Acts 28:1–10).

When you have carried out your dramatic reading, it is worthwhile reflecting on any insights you have gained either into the story or into yourself. Here are some questions that will help:

- What knowledge have I gained?
- What have I seen differently?
- How do I feel towards the character I represented?
- How do I feel towards the characters I interacted with?
- How would I alter the plot of this story and why? Can I imagine a different outcome?
- What connections are there between this story and my life situation?

In order to prepare for a presentation of the story, you can take some more steps. For instance, you can decide that the narrator, who provides continuity, will be one of the characters who appears in the story. You may also want to elaborate some of the conversations to make clearer the context of the story and the issues that are raised in it. By now, you will need to rewrite the biblical story in your own words. It is often helpful to have two people working on this together.

Then you could decide to give the people in the stories different accents. For instance, Pharaoh could be very well-spoken but with a foreign accent, Aaron could use a pious tone and Moses could have a rural accent. Finally you may want to work out some props that will convey the setting and dress. But often, especially in church settings, it is better to leave as much as possible to the imagination.

As well as such straightforward dramatization of a Bible account, there are other ways of 'playing' a biblical story. For example, you can create an imaginative development from the biblical story or, secondly, a dramatic presentation that helps you to engage with biblical issues:

- Imagine what the boy with the five loaves and a few fish would say to his mother when he arrived home after the feeding of the five thousand (see John 6:1–15). You could improvise in pairs, one being the mother and the other the boy, share your results and work on a script that includes the best ideas and lines.
- Imagine the conversations of the ten disciples gathered fearfully behind locked doors, prior to the resurrection appearance of Jesus (John 20:19–23). One way to do this is for each person in the group to become a disciple and imagine their thoughts, feelings and

reactions. What sounds would they hear and how would they respond? What were they recalling from the life of Jesus, and how were they handling the rumours of an empty tomb told by the women? Were they planning to escape from Jerusalem and what would they do then? Note some of these ideas down and then get the 'disciples' to hold a conversation among themselves.

Another imaginative approach to dramatizing a Bible story is to develop a script but transfer the context to a modern one. For example:

• Work out three stories that someone in an important national position, whether in politics, business or the Church, might tell his or her grandchildren (aged 12–15) to help them understand the temptations they have experienced. (Obviously the intention is to parallel the temptations of Jesus, which you can read in Matthew or Luke chapter 4.)
• Read the story of the prodigal son (Luke 15:11–28) with a group of adolescents. Talk about similar situations that you can envisage in our culture, then turn this into a short drama.

IN THE HOT SEAT

'Hot-seating' is a really exciting way to engage people with a Bible passage or story. People have the option of being one of various characters in a particular Bible account and of answering questions posed to them by other members of the group, as that character. One of the fundamental ground rules is that once the person in the 'hot seat' is acting as their chosen character, they alone are the judge of how that character thinks and feels, based on the facts of the story and their own imagination. The rest of the group, by asking questions of the character, stimulate the imagination of the one in the hot seat.

Here is one experienced facilitator's assessment of the process:

The value of the activity is that it turns distant people in a far-off, long-ago setting into people like us. It makes us put thoughts into their heads and words into their mouths. To do this we are forced to empathize with their situation and 'become' them for a while.

The method seems to help the questioners, i.e. the rest of the group, to raise questions to the character that wouldn't necessarily occur to them when simply looking at the text. The discussion can become quite intense but since it is with a character, not one of us, no one is hurt by personal questions. It seems too that as one person in the hot seat answers the question, the others consider how they might have answered.[1]

What these observations indicate is that people become involved with the story in several ways: by reading it or listening to it; by becoming one of the characters and seeing life through their eyes; and by putting questions to other characters.

Clearly this is not a free-fall process because the Bible story gives many indicators of what took place and so on, but not all aspects of the situation are normally set out in the text, so there is much scope for personal and group exploration.

Preparation for 'hot-seating'

- Choose the story, a relatively familiar one if possible. It may well be necessary to explain the biblical context to the group, but keep this fairly short. The important part of hot-seating is people's own involvement in the story.
- Read the story from the Bible several times, using whichever translation you feel comfortable with.
- List the main characters mentioned in the story.
- Read the story again, considering who else there might be with something to tell about the events (members of crowds, relatives of the main characters, neighbours).
- Divide the story into episodes, looking for natural breaks or points that prompt questions.
- Prepare a few questions to put to each character, in case your group takes a while to get going on its own.
- Consider how the session will end. Usually it is best to have a by-

stander or minor character in the hot seat last, to provide some kind of independent view. You could also end with a debriefing session where people are encouraged to explore what the whole experience has meant for them. This can include insights gained, emotions experienced and decisions that have been taken. Try to help people relate their experience of hot seating (both in character and as questioners) to their own real-life situations.

- Provide small props for each character to use when they are in the hot seat.

Leading

- Explain to your group that you are going to explore a Bible story by interviewing some of the people there at the time. They will hear the story read twice from the Bible. During the second reading they can get ready to volunteer to become one of the characters to sit in the hot seat and answer questions from the rest of the group.
- Read the story twice, wait until all those who want to have chosen a character, and then ask for a volunteer to take the hot seat as the first witness.
- Be prepared to open the questioning and then encourage everyone to join in. The person in the hot seat answers the question in the role to the best of their ability, but they should feel free to say 'I don't know' if necessary.
- Decide when to end a witness's contribution and move on to the next, depending on whether the witness is becoming tired or the group is getting bored or running out of questions.
- Finish either with a bystander character or a debriefing session, giving people the opportunity to share any new insights they have gained.

Example

To give you some idea of how 'In the hot seat' can work in practice, let's consider a very short story from Luke's Gospel (Luke 9:51–56). Read the passage through now.

The characters, with their props, are:
- Jesus (a cross)
- Messenger (a map)
- Samaritan villager (big bunch of keys)
- James and John (a Bible opened at 1 Kings 18)
- Woman follower (a basket)
- Bystander (a stick)

Taking the episodes in verses 51–52, and with Jesus in the hot seat, possible questions are:
- What was in your mind as you set out for Jerusalem?
- How did you decide where to spend the night?
- How did you select your messengers?
- Why did you not all march into the village?
- What did you do while you waited for the messengers to return?
- What are the messengers' names?

Using the same episodes, but with a messenger in the hot seat, questions could be:
- Why did Jesus pick you?
- What did you feel about being selected?
- What was involved in 'getting everything ready'?
- How did you expect the Samaritans to welcome you?
- What was going through your mind as you returned to report to Jesus and the other disciples?

Questions for episodes in verse 53, with a Samaritan villager in the hot seat, are:
- What was life like in your village?
- What did you feel about the Jews?
- What had you heard about Jesus?
- Why did it matter that Jesus was on his way to Jerusalem?
- How did you all decide not to let Jesus and the disciples stay?
- Can you give us a flavour of the conversation?
- How did you feel when you turned the messengers away?

Here are possible questions for episodes in verses 54–55, and with James and/or John in the hot seat. (They might even quarrel over who goes first!)

- What did you think of the Samaritans before this incident?
- How did you feel when you heard they had rejected you?
- Did you really think they deserved to be destroyed? How were you feeling at the time?
- What prompted you to think that you could call down fire on them like Elijah?
- What did you expect Jesus to say when you asked him your question?

Questions for episodes from verse 56, with a woman follower in the hot seat, are:

- How were you feeling by now—tired, hungry, rejected?
- What did the disciples look like and talk about as they trailed after Jesus?
- Why do you think Jesus reacted as he did?
- How did you respond to James' and John's concern to stand up for Jesus?

Finally, a bystander might be put in the hot seat and asked to summarize the incident from their perspective.

This is quite a difficult passage to get into, but it raises all kinds of significant issues: the purpose of Jesus' life and death; his concern to look after his disciples; inter-ethnic and religious disputes; the way we use the Bible to justify our reactions, either formally, informally or subconsciously; and the different ways in which women and men view situations.

THE MOST FAMOUS PLAY OF THEM ALL

Arguably the most famous attempt to 'play' the Bible is the Passion Play of Oberammergau.

Apparently it was in 1633 that the village elders, together with any others who could walk, made their way to the local church. Before the

high altar a solemn vow was made, that every ten years, from generation to generation for ever, they would perform this play. They would
devote themselves freely and fully to preparing for and performing 'The
tragedy of Our Lord's Passion, thus keeping the Christian principle of
the Redemption before the world, in all its trials and perplexities, for
evermore'.[2] The reason for this solemn and costly vow was that the
plague, partly sparked off by the refugee problems associated with the
Thirty Years War, had reached Oberammergau and was devastating the
population. The result of that initial vow was amazing: 'From that time
onwards, it is said, not a single death from the Plague occurred in the
village.'[3]

Every ten years since 1680 (apart from 1770 when it was prohibited
and 1940 when it was not possible) the Passion Play has been performed. But it has by no means been the same play. In 1750, for
instance, it was presented as a cosmic drama between God and Lucifer.
Now there is an intention to emphasize the humanity of Jesus, although
the chorus and prologue bring out the divine side of the Passion as well.
The play is also concerned to underline the significance of the Old
Testament, and this is one way in which it seeks to avoid the charge
of anti-Semitism which earlier versions received because of the over-
emphasis on the role of the Jews in the death of Jesus.

A radio programme I heard about Oberammergau included
interviews with those playing major parts such as Jesus and Judas. For
many months they had a heavy schedule of practice and performing,
and then, throughout the season, endless hours of performance. Normal work and life are totally disrupted for the two thousand people
involved. It is clear that repeatedly living through the Passion, as the
actors obviously do, profoundly challenges and changes those who take
part. Of course, Oberammergau has also become a huge commercial
concern, not least for the holiday trade. But in the process, the 500,000
people who attended the play in 2000 have been challenged to think
again about the significance of the life and death of Jesus.

If you, or any others in your group, have been to Oberammergau,
encourage them to recall their experiences. If not, why not find someone who has been (or, better still, a small group of people) and inter-

view them? You could do this on tape, make a video or invite them to your group. Here are some questions you could consider:

- What kind of day was it, who were you with, and how long did it all take?
- What position were you in, in relation to the stage (near or far, in front or to the side)? Could you see and hear everything?
- Do you remember any of your thoughts and feelings before the performance began? (Were you thirsty, fed up with waiting, apprehensive about the length of the play?)
- Which character remains most vividly in your mind, or to whom were you most attracted? Can you explain why this was?
- Did you think that Jesus was presented realistically? Have you gained any new insights about Jesus through this presentation?

  One mature Christian I spoke to said they had 'fallen in love with Jesus for the first time'. They didn't mean the actor (!) but the person of Jesus, who was now real enough and human enough for them to make that kind of connection.
- What about the presentation of Judas, Peter, Herod or Pilate?
- Who are the most impressive women in the story? (Until 1990 only unmarried women under 35 were allowed to act in the play!)
- In what ways do you think watching the play was different from reading the Gospel? (For example, did the storyline change; was a different 'spin' put on any characters or incidents; was anything you consider significant missed out?)
- From the perspective of the play, why did Jesus die?
- Did you gain any new insight into the gospel message?
- Has it made any significant difference to your faith or behaviour?
- What is your most abiding memory from the experience?

FURTHER AFIELD

As a follow-up, you or your group could plan to go to a theatre (or church) where there is a dramatic presentation of biblical material. Alternatively, go to Oberammergau! Even if your visit is to a local performance, you might like to ask yourselves similar questions to the ones suggested for Oberammergau.

PRAYER

Father God, we thank you that, as people made in your image, you have given us a sense of fun and enabled us to grow through playing. Help us to capture the spirit of excitement and liberation expressed by the crowds who welcomed Jesus to Jerusalem. Help us to learn to be spontaneous and yet to blend together as they did. Help us so to grow in our appreciation of scripture that it becomes natural for us to speak, sing and live it. This we ask so that your Son, Jesus Christ, may be glorified through our lives too. Amen.

Chapter 2

RE-WRITE IT

ICE-BREAKERS

1. Play a game of Dingbats together. (Dingbats is the game where common phrases are expressed by the way letters and other signs are positioned. So, if a vertical line were placed inside the letter Q, the 'dingbat' would be 'line up in a queue'.) If you wish, devise some biblical dingbats, or run a competition for the best ones for the following week.

2. Copy out a crossword on a very large scale so that it can be placed on the floor (please choose a crossword of an appropriate level of difficulty for your group). Then appoint one person as the scorer. (Alternatively, you can give each team a pen with a different coloured ink and add up the scores at the end.) Divide your group into three teams and give each team the same set of clues. The task is to write the answers on the master crossword grid on the floor.

There are several ways to play this. Either allow each team to complete a word in turn (scoring five points per letter), or allow each team to add a maximum of three letters at a time. With the second option, as well as five points per letter, the team gets an extra ten points when they complete a word. If you want a more exciting version, allow people to scramble to put letters in, again giving the bonus ten points to those who finish any word.

You can devise a penalty system for wrong answers if you want. If you are really creative, you can add an extra biblical flavour by finding or devising a Bible-based crossword. The point of this ice-breaker is, however, the process of re-writing words—that is, changing the clues into single words and, most importantly, having fun together.

3. Think about times when you have either written or read 'ghastly mistakes'. Have you come across any particularly funny ones too? Share your recollections as a group.

INTRODUCTION

When people rewrite something, there are many ways they can do it. Clearly, they can copy down something already in writing, as I might copy one of the 'Poems on the Underground', where, on tube trains, instead of the usual advertisements for travel insurance and deodorants a piece of poetry is printed on a poster. Equally, if someone rewrites a well-known fairy story, they could add their own embellishments, or an artist could provide vivid pictures that give new vitality to the old account. Rewriting, in terms of copying out, has been crucial for the survival of the Bible. When the Bible is translated, or translated again and again, as is the case with English language versions, then it is more like a new version of an old story. This too has been vital for spreading the message of the Bible. Sometimes, as we shall see, these processes have led to some amusing outcomes.

Within the Bible, we can read of passages being rewritten. In the case of Moses' infamous re-writing of the Ten Commandments, this was necessary because he had destroyed the originals in anger at God's people (Deuteronomy 9:8—10:5. Do we ever have the right to with-hold God's word from other people?)

In Jeremiah's case he rewrote part of his prophecies because some-one destroyed the originals in an attempt to neutralize the power of God's word (Jeremiah 36). Are you aware of any countries or organizations who would like to silence the Bible today?

These biblical examples are drawn from very serious situations, but rewriting can be a very creative and enjoyable endeavour. Following the Bible Study we will introduce a few ways to do this, but first we will look in more detail at one of the ways in which part of the Bible was rewritten.

BIBLE STUDY

Read Luke 1:1–4.

In these opening verses, known as the Prologue, Luke uses wonderful Greek (it's the nearest to classical Greek in the New Testament) and he is wonderfully polite—after all, he is probably writing to a high-ranking Roman official called Theophilus (although this may well be a pseudonym to protect the real person: it means 'lover of God') and wanting to persuade him to take an interest in Jesus. Luke also wishes to establish that Jesus' followers are decent people and unlikely to cause disturbances. In the process he tells us that he is doing a serious rewrite of all the material about Jesus that he has come across (including the Gospels of Matthew and Mark), in order to ensure that Theophilus receives an orderly and full account of everything he has been taught. Clearly Luke is sure he can improve on what has gone before!

- Do you agree that Luke's Gospel is an improvement on Mark and Matthew, or do you like one of those two better? Share your reasons and reflections with one another.
- Can you spot any places where Luke has changed the order of events in comparison with the other Gospels?
- Luke intends to give a more relevant and comprehensive account than others then available. Has any person, any book, any video, any Bible translation done this for you? Share your thoughts with one another.
- What are the risks in 'rewriting' to make the message more acceptable for a different audience? What safeguards does Luke suggest we should try to use?
- Look at four or more translations of Luke 1:1-4; or a story in Luke,

such as Luke 2:1–20 or 24:13–35; or Luke's account of a story Jesus told, for instance Luke 10:30–35 or 15:11–32. A varied set of translations would be the Authorized Version, the New Jerusalem Bible, the Contemporary English Version and finally a paraphrase such as THE MESSAGE by Eugene Peterson. Discuss which you think works best and why. You may also find it interesting to read the prefaces or introductions to the translations to understand what each translation was attempting to do. Ask yourself whether you think they achieved their aims.

- Do you think one translation works best for all types of material in the Bible, for every situation—personal reading, study, reading aloud in church—and for all kinds of people—mature Christian and recent convert, those with differing levels of reading ability, or different personality types?

In the rest of this chapter we shall look at several different ways of rewriting the Bible. Some appear to keep much closer to the words of the Bible than others, but remember that we are working from translations anyway. We might also consider the issue of whether God is more concerned with the 'purity of the text' or with people getting the message. What do you think?

COPYING

There have been some unfortunate mistakes made in copying the Bible:

- The so-called 'Wicked' edition of the Bible, published in 1632, missed out a very significant 'not'—in the seventh commandment in Exodus 20:14. The verse makes interesting reading without it!
- Another lost 'not' meant that the 'unrighteous' were promised that they would inherit the kingdom in 1 Corinthians 6:9.
- Every Bible has its printers, but the 1702 Printers' Bible became notorious. Psalm 119:161 read, 'Printers (rather than princes) have persecuted me without a cause.'

- Finally, 'peacemakers' were replaced by 'placemakers' in Matthew 5:9 in a Geneva Bible of 1562.[4]

This all goes to show that it isn't as easy as you might think to produce an absolutely accurate text—so have a go!

Copy out John 1:1–10 or Luke 3:23–38 by hand. Afterwards talk together about how you found it—easy or difficult—and why. Now check one another's copies: at least two people should check each copy. Have you learnt anything about this kind of rewriting the Bible?

Take time to thank God for the thousands of people who, over many centuries, have worked tirelessly to copy the text of the Bible as faithfully as possible. It is itself a wonder of the ancient world!

One area of biblical criticism is known as 'textual criticism'. This compares all known manuscripts, which sometimes, as with a fragment from John's Gospel, go back to within a few decades of when the books were written. This kind of study has established that there has been an amazing level of accuracy in the rewriting of the Bible. When large sections of the Old Testament (in Hebrew, of course) were discovered at Qumran, near the Dead Sea, in the middle of the 20th century, they were almost a thousand years older than previously known manuscripts. They confirmed to an almost unbelievable extent that the copying of the text had gone on down the centuries with very few changes or errors creeping in.

This is a good prompt to pray for those who today are involved in preparing the text for new versions of the Bible.

CALLIGRAPHY

If thousands of people had not spent years copying out the Bible, we might well not have it today. For 1500 years after the New Testament was written, this was the main way in which the Bible was preserved.

Try to work out how long it would take you to copy out the whole Bible by hand. (A quick way of doing this is to copy out half a page from your Bible and multiply the time it takes to do this, in minutes, by twice the number of pages in the Bible; then divide your answer by 60 to find the total time in hours.) Many of those who carried out this task for real would have taken many times longer, partly because they worked with incredible care and partly because their equipment would have slowed them down—they would have needed to keep sharpening their quills and even make their own ink. One of the early manuscripts of the New Testament, probably around 1600 years old, is the *Codex Sinaiticus*, which is kept at the British Library, London. Even though it is handwritten, amazingly all the letters are the same size. It looks just as though it has been printed. Imagine how long it would take you to copy the Bible this carefully! But many manuscripts are even more amazing, because many of the pages are works of art as well. A famous example of these 'illuminated manuscripts' is the Lindisfarne Gospels. Try to borrow a library book showing the sort of work that was produced. Alternatively, get hold of postcards or pictures that illustrate these manuscripts. Discuss among yourselves how this makes you feel and why you think people invested so much time and creative energy in this kind of rewriting.

• Have a go! Form groups of about four people—each group preferably including someone with some artistic skills or experience of calligraphy. Alternatively, use a computer to explore different fonts and drawing, painting and desk-top publishing programmes. Then decide on a verse that you would like to 'illuminate'.

   Do you want to do it in the medieval style, with pictures (although remember that these pictures were themselves more like a symbolic code than straightforward reproductions of everyday objects), or in a more modern, perhaps abstract style? Share ideas about how to enhance or bring out the meaning of your text. Then do it!

   Finally, find a way to share with others your work and the experience of doing it—perhaps as an article in your church newsletter or even an exhibition! Alternatively, have your artwork reproduced as a postcard, poster or birthday card.

• Another way to explore rewriting is to get hold of a copy of George Herbert's poem 'Easter Wings', in which the layout of the lines reflects the image of the poem. Overleaf is one of the verses to give you the 'picture'. (Spelling has been modernized.)

My tender age in sorrow did begin:
And still with sicknesses and shame
Thou didst so punish sin,
That I became
Most thin.
With thee
Let me combine
And feel this day thy victory:
For, if I imp my wing on thine,
Affliction shall advance the flight in me.

The shape of the stanza is that of a pair of wings, or a butterfly. Can you think of any Bible passages which could be laid out with a distinctive shape that matches the message?

CULTURAL ADAPTATIONS

Every translation is, to some extent, a cultural adaptation. If there is no awareness of snow in a tropical rainforest area, how do you translate 'as white as snow' for the people who live there? If people have never seen a sheep, how do you explain about a shepherd? But cultural adaptation can go much further. Here is one way in which one of the most famous passages in the Bible—1 Corinthians 13—has been rewritten.

Language student preparing for overseas missions work

If I know the language ever so perfectly and speak like a pundit and have not the love that grips the heart, I am nothing. If I have decorations and diplomas and am proficient in up-to-date methods, and have not the touch of understanding love, I am nothing.

If I have all the faith and great ideals and magnificent plans and wonderul visions, and have not the love that sweats and bleeds and prays and weeps and pleads, I am nothing.

If I surrender all prospects and, leaving home and friends and comforts,

give myself to the showy sacrifice of a missionary career, and turn sour and selfish amid the daily annoyances and personal slights of a missionary life, and though I give my body to be consumed in the heat and sweat and mildew of India, and have not the love that yields its rights, its coveted leisure, its pet plans, I am nothing. Nothing. Virtue has ceased to go out from me.
SOURCE UNKNOWN

Here are some ideas to think about in relation to this passage:

* Spot two phrases or words or images that reflect the special perspective of the writer.
* Note three or more phrases that capture your imagination, and think about why this is so.
* What special insights have you gained from this 'translation'? Are there phrases which annoy you or you think misrepresent the Bible passage? If so, note them down.

Now share your views together.

The next step is to do your own 'rewrite'. Decide on a type of person or group of people that you know well—young mothers, a farmer, a senior citizens' club, keep-fit enthusiasts, clubbers—and choose another well-known passage to rewrite from their perspective, such as Psalm 23 or Luke 10:30–35.

Some points to check are:

* How well does your rewrite fit the intended audience?
* Did you manage to transfer all the points from the original?
* Are there phrases or images or words that still feel foreign to the new context?
* Do you understand the passage better through this transfer process? What has come alive for you? What puzzles you?

Finally, field-test your passage with the chosen audience! Of course, you can always rewrite it in the light of their comments—or, perhaps better still, ask them to have a go themselves.

THE BIBLE IN MINIATURE

I really like this succinct summary of the Bible, called 'The Bible in fifty words'.

God made
Adam bit
Noah arked
Abraham split,
Jacob fooled
Joseph ruled
Bush talked
Moses balked
Pharaoh plagued
People walked
Sea divided
Tablets guided
Promise landed
Saul freaked
David peeked
Prophets warned
Jesus born
God walked
Love talked
Anger crucified
Hope died
Love rose
Spirit flamed
Word spread
God remained

SOURCE UNKNOWN

Can you do better? Why not try to summarize Paul's letters along the same lines?

DIALECTS

A variant of cultural adaptation is to rewrite the Bible using dialect. Again, it has the advantage of creating a fresh interest in the Bible and helping people to feel that the Bible belongs with them.

Here is a passage from Luke 10:38–40, according to *The Geordie Bible* (privately published, 1995).

Noo for al the' wor sistors Mary and Martha wor as different as chaalk and cheese.

Martha wez the busy one. Aalwis taalkin. Aaalwis workin. Nivvor sat doon. Nee mattor when ye called she had hor pinny on…

Mary wez the quiet one. She nivvor said much. She wez aalwis sittin with a byeuk in her hand.

Wey ye kna hoo it is. If yor aalwis runnin aboot like a scadded cat and sumbody else is sittin deein nowt, it can git on yer narves. That suntimes happened te Martha…

Note how strange this seems (unless you come from the north-east!)

How would you transfer a similar passage into a dialect that is prevalent around you?

Could you organize a 'dialect Bible' competition in one of your local schools? Your local paper could well be interested in hearing about your attempt. National and international media covered the story of Mike Coles, the head of RE at a school in East London who wrote *The Bible in Cockney* (BRF, 2001).

COMMUNITY BIBLES

Do you make lists? Some people make shopping lists or lists of tasks they need to do. While it can be useful to have a list, I find that the actual writing of the list is even better. The process of writing makes me think about the issues and then helps me to remember what needs to be done. Having written the list, I can almost throw it away!

One useful and enjoyable way to 'rewrite' the Bible is to organize a local 'Community Bible'. The idea is to get as many people as possible to write out one verse of the Bible—usually from one of the Gospels—and to do so in order. The end product is a 'hand-copy' of the Gospel. Through this process it's to be hoped that people will think again about not only the individual verse but the importance of the Bible, and they may well remember the verse that they write.

Bible Society are able to supply a pack which includes high-quality paper and a commitment to bind your copy in leather so that it can be presented to the Town Hall or the Central Library. This means that your handwritten copy will stimulate others to think about the value of the Bible for society as well as the individual. Bible Society suggest that the Mayor or an equivalent person starts the process off, and that people pay £1 for each verse they write. The money raised is then used, via Bible Society, to make many more copies of the Bible available in other countries where it is still in great demand and often scarce. Hence this is a very useful way of rewriting the Bible.

If you would like more details of this scheme, then write to Bible Society for a free *Project Guide* (see Resources section for contact details, p. 154). This guide has all kinds of innovative and practical ideas to help you to get started and to complete your rewriting of the Gospel. It also has illustrations of how this has been done in other towns and cities.

FURTHER AFIELD

Why not arrange to visit the British Library and look at some of their priceless Bible manuscripts? In their bookshop you can buy copies of their beautifully illuminated manuscript pages and a copy of Tyndale's New Testament in the original spelling but in a modern script. Two things surprised me about this when I saw the original. First, the size—it was designed as a pocket book so that the ploughboy could carry it around in his pouch and read it in his lunch break. Second, God is always written 'god'.

Your nearest cathedral may also have a collection of Bible manuscripts which would be worth a visit. Sometimes these are on display and sometimes you will need to make prior arrangements to see them.

To share your experience, plan a party for some friends where you talk about your visit to the city and include reference to the cathedral, maybe using photographs you have taken or even a video show. The fact that you bothered to go on a day out to find out more about the Bible may well challenge your guests to think that this book could matter to them as well. However, make sure it's a good party if you want them to have a more positive attitude to the Bible (see Chapter 5).

PRAYER

Living God, we thank you that you have entrusted your message to us through the scriptures. We thank you for the many people who, over thousands of years, have seen what you have done and listened to what you said and have left us the written record. Thank you too for those who, over the last two thousand years, have ensured that we can still read the great story of your revelation to us. Now help us, creatively and faithfully, to pass on the precious and life-giving truth we have received. Bless those who will discover your ways through all that we do now. Amen.

Chapter 3

DISPLAY IT

ICE-BREAKERS

1. Share your experiences of art or craft at school—including what the art teacher was like.
2. If you are a parent or grandparent, what is it like receiving the gift of a child's drawing? Think about the opportunities for building or destroying self-esteem that surround such a gift. What positive or painful memories do you have of how your attempts to draw as a child were regarded by others?
3. Who is your favourite artist and why? Have you ever been to an art gallery to see any of that artist's original works? Share your views and experiences.
4. Think about ads, especially on the TV. Which do you reckon is the most memorable and why? Is it the storyline, the photography, the music, the words, the images? Is advertising a perversion of art (in its widest sense) as it uses art to sell products?

INTRODUCTION

The Bible is a very vivid book. Not only does it contain some of the most memorable stories in the world, but within it there is a great emphasis on the visual sense and its significance. For instance, right at the beginning with the creation story in Genesis 1, we read repeatedly, 'God was pleased with what he *saw*' (my emphasis) and the book of Revelation is full of colourful, even disturbing, visions. At the centre of our faith, and the Bible, is the appearance of Jesus: John's Gospel makes the comment, 'We *saw* his glory' (my emphasis). In this chapter we are going to explore some ways in which we can release the visual potential of the Bible, and in so doing discover how our own appreciation of it has grown. First, we are going to look at a Bible passage in which a variety of artistic gifts are affirmed.

BIBLE STUDY

This study is based on Exodus 35:4—40:38.

Life in the wilderness could be pretty drab—manna to eat day after day and little change of scenery from rocks and sand. But there were two things designed to relieve the visual boredom. The first was the 'Tent of meeting' or 'Tent of the Lord's Presence' or, as it used to be called in older versions, the 'Tabernacle'. The second was the 'dazzling light of the Lord's presence' or 'the 'glory of the Lord' which filled the Tent when God was present, so much so that Moses did not go into it at those times.

Chapters 35—40 of Exodus are all devoted to the amazing construction of this Tent. By all means read the six chapters, especially if you are either an architect or have a fascination with interior design. Alternatively, you could read a small selection to give yourself a flavour: for instance, 36:8–38 gives the core of it, describing a wonderfully crafted construction, glowing with blue, purple and red, shimmering with gold and silver.

What is striking about these chapters (see 35:30—36:1 in particular) is the way that artistic resources are affirmed as a means of honouring God. Here there is no dour puritanism forbidding the use of colour and artistic expression; there is no trace of any command forbidding the application of creative gifts to stimulate the imagination.

Indeed such creativity is attributed to the Spirit of God: of Bezalel it is said, 'God has filled him with his Spirit[5] and given him skill, ability, and under-standing for every kind of artistic work, for planning skilful designs and working them in gold, silver and bronze; for cutting jewels to be set; for carving wood; and for every other kind of artistic work' (Exodus 35:31–33).

Here is a very direct and clear recognition that such gifts come from God: whether the imaginative ability, or the planning, or the construction of the design, all are from God. Equally, working with all kinds and combinations of materials is affirmed. What a rich tapestry! And all of it is acceptable to build the chosen place for God to dwell. You cannot get much better affirmation of the arts than this. But there is one more step—the ability to teach others also (35:34).

I also find the depiction of the people bringing their gifts for the building of the Tabernacle interesting. For me, two things stand out. First, although not all have such artistic gifts as Bezalel and his colleague Oholiab, all can contribute by providing materials. Second, the artistic vision seems to have been enormously motivational: 'All the people who wanted to brought their offering to the Lord for the work which he had commanded Moses to do' (35:29). Moses had to call a halt to the giving. Now how often does that happen for a church appeal? And don't forget that they were stranded in the desert.

So here is a remarkable affirmation that the creative arts can be a gift from God, and that they can be used to honour the reality of God and help others worship God more fully. Here too is a model of how all can work together to produce something that is pleasing to God.

Before we move on to look at how such gifts can be used to 'display' the Bible, let's reflect on our own experience of worship in the light of this Old Testament passage.

Can you think of an event in your church (or any church) where you came away thinking, 'That was amazing—I really felt God's presence in that... exhibition... flower festival...'?

Reflect on whether anyone with artistic gifts ever tried to pass on their skill and understanding to you. How did you respond? Have you ever thought of doing the same?

What materials can you work in—fabrics (including embroidery), metal, wood, plastic, glass, paint, oils, crayons? Why do you like working in this medium?

Talk about opportunities you may have had (and if so, whether you took them) to use those skills to express some biblical truth.

Which church or cathedral building do you find best helps you to worship God? What particular features help you?

Why not do an audit of your church to see just how many skills are displayed there, and reflect on what they can teach us about our faith?

- The architecture—including the position and the shape of the church. Are these significant?
- The furniture: where is the pulpit, the altar/communion table, font/baptistry, pews/chairs? Are there kneelers?
- What decoration is there—texts, stained-glass windows, murals, carvings, sculptures, banners, posters? Why were they given—and what do they say about the relationships the church has with groups and individuals?
- How many different styles and periods are reflected in your church building? Does this contribute to or detract from worship, as far as you are concerned?
- What do the furniture and architecture say about the overall conception of your building (is it a temple, a theatre, a meeting-house, a lecture hall) and the corresponding view of God?
- Can you share an occasion when you felt that God was really in this place? If so, please try to share that experience with your group.

Now let's take what we have gleaned from a quick trip round the Tabernacle in the wilderness and our home church and apply it to the challenge of encountering the Bible for ourselves.

DRAW AND PAINT

There are many straightforward ways to relate to the Bible through these approaches. Below are some variations which should add an additional level of interest.

CARTOONS

Cartoons can be used to illustrate characters or bring out the humour, or (in a daily newspaper style) to depict a biblical event. If you pursue this idea as a group, it could be helpful to collect a wide range of examples, from different newspapers for instance, and think together about how the artists are achieving their effects. You could work together on some humorous and some serious attempts of your own, with some members helping to choose the subjects, others doing the drawing and still others coming up with snappy captions. If you want to give continuity to your group of cartoons, you can do this by having a common theme, or by basing all the cartoons on one book of the Bible.

If you enjoy this approach and want to become more ambitious, why not produce a book of cartoons? (This could be produced using a photocopier.) Perhaps you could organize this among the churches of the town, or in your diocese or district. In the process you might discover some real talent—you should certainly have a good laugh.

If you want to see how other people deal with biblical subjects, there is a series of cards with cartoons by Steve Best under the name 'Bestie', which show one approach. But many Christian books also have cartoons which will stimulate your own approaches.

Another way to use this idea is to organize a competition, perhaps with different subjects and/or different age groups.

Alternatively, as your skills and confidence develop, you could offer to illustrate the Bible passages being used each Sunday in your church. Your cartoons could either be displayed on an overhead projector while the readings take place, or they could be reproduced as part of the order of service. They could even be turned into posters to attract people to the church and its message.

ARTS AND CRAFTS

A wider range of arts and crafts can also be used to illustrate biblical materials. Older Bibles, with their line drawings or coloured pictures, often provide stimulation here, but please do not restrict yourself to 'realistic representations' of Jesus or biblical subjects. Religious Christmas cards are another resource. If yours include reproductions of 'old masters', think about the extent to which the artists colour the scene with their own culture, sometimes even putting people they know into the picture.

As with the cartoons above, it is worth thinking about how to use the results of your artistic endeavours, as well as recognizing that the very process of engaging creatively with biblical materials is a way of discovering new significance in the Bible. Recently a church organized a competition for artists to produce a work to express the meaning of a Bible text, and offered a prize of £1,000! They then arranged for an art exhibition and involved the local media too. In this way, people who would not normally spend much time with the Bible were profoundly involved with its message.

If you go down this kind of route, then select a theme or verse that has relevance in our culture. For instance, 'God was pleased with what he saw' (Genesis 1:25) speaks of the beauty and fascination of creation; 'An argument broke out...' (Luke 22:24) asks the question, 'Is conflict always about power and greatness?' and 'Give us today the food we need' (Matthew 6:11) raises issues about what we need, and responsibility to others. Each of these verses is visually evocative and raises intricate issues way beyond the surface theme, providing opportunities for creative artists to explore through their visual medium.

Church holiday clubs for children have made much use of crafts as a way of exploring and expressing the significance of Bible stories. Adults could be challenged to express abstract biblical ideas such as love, grace, justice, forgiveness, hope or truth using cardboard boxes and empty plastic bottles. This could make an excellent activity for a 'Light Party'—the Christian alternative to Halloween which is growing in popularity. One way to do it is to put people in small groups, let them pick a theme out of a hat, then work at it for 30 minutes, with five minutes for each group to explain their 'creation' to everyone at the end. If space permits, the models could be left around the church until the following weekend for everyone to see.

VISUAL IMAGES

- Draw an outline of a human body and get people to discuss and then draw (and name) different functions within the life of the church: who is the mouth (preachers, people who always speak at meetings); who are the hands (the fabric committee, the caterers, the cleaners, or the prayer group)? Do this for each of the main components of the body (see 1 Corinthians 12—14).
- Pick another visual image of the church or Christian people that is used in the Bible, and explore its importance in a similar way: for example, the lamp (Matthew 5:14–16), the soldier (Ephesians 6:12–17; 2 Timothy 2:3–4), the garden (1 Corinthians 3:6–9), the building (Ephesians 2:21–22; 1 Peter 2:5).
- Investigate a biblical theme or image and produce a series of sketches (either one each on pieces of A4, which you can arrange into an order, or using the reverse side of some wallpaper to produce a visual scroll). Some starter ideas for themes are growth, mountains, storms and boats, or justice. You can do this either individually or as a group. It may well be that once you have gained some competence, you can offer to enhance special services, such as Harvest festivals, Life Boat services, or a service for Christian Aid.

WINDOWS

If your church has stained-glass windows depicting biblical stories or themes, how could you help visitors to the church to appreciate the windows more (or, indeed, other visual aspects of the building)? For instance, what about producing a leaflet or commentary cassette, including a relevant Bible portion to introduce people to the bigger story?

If your church has a website, could you arrange for photographs of the stained glass to be put on the site with links to Bible passages?

FLOWER FESTIVAL

Flower festivals are another way to unpack some biblical themes. They have one strong advantage and one definite disadvantage.

Disadvantage

Flower festivals are a lot of work (even if you really love flower arranging and find it creative, therapeutic and social) and the results only last a few days—as indeed the Bible itself reminds us on several occasions (see Psalm 90:5–6; 103:15–16; Matthew 6:29–30). There are a few extras, however, that can ensure the impact lasts longer and, don't forget, the memory of those flowers, especially if they are expressing a biblical truth, can last for ever: 'Yes, grass withers and flowers fade, but the word of our God endures for ever' (Isaiah 40:8).

Advantage

Flower festivals are very popular, especially if you live in some kind of tourist spot or in a busy neighbourhood, and particularly if you offer refreshments!

- They entice people into the church building, where, if those on duty are warm and friendly, people may want to come again, having once ventured over the threshold.
- People tend to linger and reflect on the displays, which means that God's truth can sink in and reach the parts that other methods seldom reach. This can be fostered by having a leaflet explaining the significance of the whole festival and the relevance of each display.
- Visitors may stop to pray or pick up a piece of Christian literature, and who knows what God will do then?

- The flower displays can help people to make, even if at an unconscious level, the connection between God and beauty, creation and Creator.

While the impact on visitors is primary, I believe that in terms of engaging with the Bible the impact on those staging the festival may be even greater.

SOME BASICS TO REMEMBER

Decide on a good time for the event (availability of flowers and the building are starting points, but also bear in mind the availability of people to take part).

Decide on the theme (more on this later), work out where each arrangement can be placed, preferably ensuring that visitors can move easily from one to another and that each site is appropriate for its subject (don't put 'death' next to the font, unless you are intending to make a dramatic point in a challenging way!). You need to bear in mind available lighting (natural or artificial).

If you do not have enough skilled flower arrangers in your church, then involve others, either from other churches or from secular flower-arranging clubs. You may well discover that some of your members are in such clubs already and this gives them the opportunity to welcome club friends into the Christian community.

SELECTING THE THEME

If the festival is planned for Easter, Pentecost or Christmas, then to some extent the theme will be predetermined, although even here there is huge scope for creativity. If you have chosen another time, then the following examples will give you some ideas for themes.

Family

- Adam and Eve: When all was bright and beautiful
- Abraham, Sarah and Isaac: Sacrifice and God's provision

- Naomi, Ruth and Boaz: Sorrow and joy
- Joseph, Mary and Jesus: Devotion to God
- Jairus, his daughter and wife: Healing/new life
- Mary, Martha and Lazarus: Open home and hearts
- Lois, Eunice and Timothy: A believing family

A Psalm (for example, number 103)

- Verses 1–2: Praise—all my being
- Verses 3–5: Forgiveness—the soaring eagle
- Verses 6–7: Favouring the oppressed—deliverance from Egypt
- Verses 8–14: The kindness of God—as high as the sky
- Verses 15–18: A contrasting pair—brevity and stability
- Verse 19: The Lordship of God—a throne in heaven
- Verses 20–22: Praise—all creatures

Light and darkness

- At creation (Genesis 1:14–19)
- At Sinai (Exodus 19:16–22)
- The light of the world (Matthew 5:13–16)
- At the cross (Matthew 27:45)
- The world and the church (Philippians 2:14–16)
- Endless light (Revelation 21:23–24)

A Gospel

Take people through the whole story, with a display on some of the following:

- Birth
- Childhood of Jesus
- Baptism and temptations
- Teaching
- Healing

- Triumphal entry into Jerusalem
- Crucifixion
- Resurrection

Parables

Portray some of the parables, or take one parable and develop themes.
For example:

- The Good Samaritan (Luke 11:29–37): Who is my neighbour?
  - The journey
  - The robbery
  - The avoidance
  - The rescue
  - The recovery
  - The challenge

- The father and his two sons (Luke 15:11–32)
  - The departure
  - The reckless living
  - The poverty
  - The return
  - The welcome celebration
  - The pain and rejection (of the older brother)
  - Lost and found?

The seven 'I am' sayings

- Bread (John 6:48)
- Light (John 9:5)
- Door (John 10:9)
- Shepherd (John 10:11)
- Resurrection (John 11:25)
- Way, truth and life (John 14:6)
- True vine (John 15:1)

Paul's letter to the Romans

As a real challenge, I will leave it to you to pick out the main points for illustration!

MORE THAN MEETS THE EYE

There are many ways in which people can encounter the Bible through taking part in a flower festival:

* In selecting a theme, people will be thinking about different passages and discovering the broad nature of the Bible and its wide relevance to many aspects of life.
* In planning the layout of the displays, they will be exploring many aspects of the themes from a creative and imaginative angle.
* When people plan their individual display, they will be engaging with the theme in some depth as they work out how best to communicate that particular issue through colour, texture, style, shape and even smell.
* When they construct their display, people will have a prolonged encounter with their theme at a very deep level, as they struggle to express the realities they are glimpsing.
* As people care for the displays throughout the duration of the festival, they will have another opportunity to absorb their messages.
* If a leaflet is prepared to help people understand with their minds and hearts what is being 'said' through the festival, the writers will also be challenged by the Bible's message as they translate vision into text.
* Others (often husbands—I know!) will be involved in buying and transporting flowers and all the other paraphernalia. They too will have indelibly imprinted on their memories that some people at least find the Bible a source of creative inspiration.
* Finally, people will share the experience of dismantling the displays and reviewing the whole festival, including perhaps writing a report and so gathering viewers' comments.

ADDED VALUE

The disadvantage we noted about a flower festival is that the 'show' only lasts a few days. Here are some ideas to extend its impact.

- Invite a local art class or club or school to paint the flower displays and then mount an exhibition. You could offer a prize.
- Then, get the local paper or even radio station to come down and do a feature on the festival. If you know someone who is good at journalism, you could ask them to write up the story and submit it. It helps to include photographs.
- You could even go one step further and run a photographic competition. Again, do this in partnership with a local photographic society (or camera shop) and put on a display in the local library or other community building.

FURTHER AFIELD

Visit a national or local art gallery and look out for pictures that convey biblical themes (you may be able to consult their catalogue and arrange to see pictures which are not on exhibition), or visit a church that has striking stained-glass windows or other visual features. Either just enjoy the trip or, if you want to do more work afterwards, discuss together (or ask yourself):

- What were those who painted, put together the display or designed the stained glass attempting to communicate?
- How easy is it to make sense of the images or pictures without a prior knowledge of the incidents or stories depicted?
- If this was the only way you knew the story of the Bible:
  - What view of God would you have?
  - What would you know about the life of Jesus?
  - What would you think about Jesus?
- Does seeing the Bible through art make the Bible less or more relevant for you today?

PRAYER

All: *For every sign of your creative gifts, we praise you, Holy Spirit.*

Leader: *For homely chapels, beautiful churches and imposing cathedrals, for their architecture, art and music, and for the people past and present who worship in them, we thank you.*

All: *For every sign of your creative gifts, we praise you, Holy Spirit.*

Leader: *For all people, whether television personalities or our families and friends, who through design, painting, photography and flowers can communicate deep things to our souls, we thank you.*

All: *For every sign of your creative gifts, we praise you, Holy Spirit.*

Leader: *For all the skills that we can share and for all the presentations the Bible inspires, we thank you.*

All: *Amen, Amen, Amen.*

Chapter 4

EAT IT

ICE-BREAKERS

1. Invite each person to think of a special meal they have attended in the last six months, such as a wedding banquet, a birthday celebration, a farewell meal, a company or graduation dinner, or family gathering. Share with each other the nature of the event and reflect on whether it was the special food, the surroundings, the people or the occasion that made it so memorable.
2. If you have ever been to a foreign country, what was the strangest food you have ever eaten? Was it strange because it was something completely different, or because it was something you would not normally think of eating?
3. Hands up—who's a vegetarian and who's not? Invite people to explain why, but generate a conversation rather than an argument. Does the Bible figure in the conversation?
4. Macdonald's, Little Chef, Harry Ramsden, Burger King—who thinks chain restaurants are a good thing? Why—or why not?

INTRODUCTION

Meals play a big part in the Bible. There is, of course, the famous 'first bite' of the fruit of the tree in Genesis 3, about which Milton wrote in *Paradise Lost* (Book 1):

> *Whose mortal taste*
> *Brought death into the world, and all our woe,*
> *With loss of Eden.*

Then there is the Last Supper, the final meal that Jesus ate with his disciples before his crucifixion, which forms the basis of the Church's celebration of the Eucharist or Holy Communion. Actually, it wasn't Jesus' last meal on earth (see Luke 24:38–44) and it certainly wasn't the last time that meals played an important and sometimes controversial part in the life of the early Church. Think, for example, of the issue of food distribution (Acts 6), class distinction and greed in Corinth (1 Corinthians 11:17–22), or the problem of Jews who wouldn't eat with Gentiles (Galatians 2:11–14).

The fascinating thing is that, in the Bible, 'eating' the word of God is a powerful metaphor—or even experience, in the case of the prophet Ezekiel. This seems a strange picture to us, so let's take a look at three passages in some detail to help us understand its power.

BIBLE STUDY

EZEKIEL 2:8—3:15 AND PSALM 119:103–104

Ezekiel's origins were in Jerusalem, but his message was targeted on those who had been taken into exile by the victorious Babylonian army. Ezekiel's prophecies were significantly shaped by the visions and other experiences he underwent. These used to be referred to by scholars as 'bizarre', but for those of us who are more familiar with contemporary forms of visual and musical communications, who are at home in the worlds of science-fiction and computer games, where one scene melts into another, they seem far more tame! Nevertheless, Ezekiel does record some strange things, one of which comes at the beginning of his book and probably at the beginning of his ministry as a prophet.

After God has gained Ezekiel's attention (2:1–2) and warned him to listen carefully to everything he has to say, God adds, 'And now, Ezekiel, open your mouth and eat what I am going to give you' (2:8). The passage continues with what must have been a great surprise to Ezekiel:

Just then, I saw a hand stretched out towards me. And in it was a scroll. The hand opened the scroll, and both sides of it were filled with words of sadness, mourning, and grief. The Lord said, 'Ezekiel, son of man, after you eat this scroll, go and speak to the people of Israel.' He handed me the scroll and said, 'Eat this and fill your stomach with it.' So I ate the scroll, and it tasted sweet as honey. (Ezekiel 2:9—3:1, CEV)

In some ways this recalls a spy thriller, where the spy has to eat the message, once he has memorized it, to ensure that it does not fall into the wrong hands. However, the significance for Ezekiel is different. One commentator puts it like this:

The eating of the scroll was associated with the command to go and speak the words of God to the house of Israel… Implicit in the reception of God's word, symbolized by the eating of the scroll, was the acceptance of the responsibility to utter it at God's direction. [6]

Do you see anything more in it than this? One of the surprising insights that Ezekiel gives us is that although the message was clearly unpalatable, the scroll tasted like 'honey'. Why do you think that was?

One of the psalmists uses the same imagery:

Your teachings are sweeter than honey.
They give me understanding and make me hate all lies.
(Psalm 119:103–104, CEV)

Imagine a world without sugar or sweeteners—no chocolate, toffee, fudge, jam, marmalade, biscuits, cakes or doughnuts, and that's just for starters. To get a better feel for this, go through a supermarket magazine and, with a thick felt-tip pen, cross out all the pictures of food, or anything else, that contains sugar. This was the world of the Old Testament, so this is one reason why 'your words are like honey' was such a powerful simile.

According to Ecclesiasticus 39:26 (in the Apocrypha), honey is a necessity of life—a view with which Pooh Bear, and maybe the psalmist, would concur.

However, honey was not only for the palate—it had other important values. For instance, it gave a great boost of energy (see Proverbs 16:24) —perhaps their equivalent to the chocolate bar. It was also important for medicine, soothing wounds and healing the body.

For the psalmist, then, the Law was a source of great delight and pleasure, something to be savoured and longed for, something that would keep him healthy. It was also, because of its rarity, something greatly valued (see Ezekiel 16:13). He would also know that his homeland had been described by God as a 'land flowing with milk and honey' (for example, Exodus 3:8; Numbers 13:27; Deuteronomy 6:3, NIV), so it was connected with the good things of God's promises.

There is a further element in this picture, however, to do with the sensory nature of eating honey. It clings to the mouth, and its flavour can be tasted long after it has been swallowed.

- Are there passages of scripture—a verse, a story or proverb—which you would want to describe as 'like honey'? Why not share these with one another in your group? Are they in some way sweet (encouraging, enjoyable), energizing (motivating, inspiring), or healing (in body, mind and heart)? Were they an affirming and generous gift from a friend? Or an unexpected treasure, like coming across an old bees' nest full of honey? Perhaps you regard them as honey because you only discovered them after risk and effort, like taking honey from a hive.
- If you were trying to convey the same significance about the Bible to someone today, what kind of picture or analogy would you use?
- Read through the rest of this psalm and note other 'pictures' which are used to convey the appreciation that the psalmist has for the Law. Which of these pictures do you consider the most powerful or clear?

- If you were designing an advert for honey, how would you communicate its various qualities? What kind of storyline would you follow? Could this work for promoting the value of the Bible too?

JOHN 6:25–58: THE FEEDING OF THE 5000

The feeding of the 5000 (actually 5000 plus women and children—see Matthew 14:21) is one of the few miracles to be recorded in all four Gospels. This is one way to underline its importance, although John does this in his own particular way too. He seems to select his miracles, which he calls 'signs', to link with and make real the claims that Jesus makes about himself.

'You won't live unless you eat the flesh and drink the blood of the Son of Man… My flesh is the true food, and my blood is the true drink' (John 6:53, 55, CEV). The feeding of the 5000 is the miracle that illustrates this saying about 'eating my flesh' and establishes Jesus' claim, 'I am the bread of life' (John 6:48).

The miracle happens because the crowd, impressed by the many healing miracles of Jesus, follow him across the Lake of Galilee. John points out that it was almost Passover time—the time when Israel celebrated her deliverance from Egypt and also the provision of manna by God when they were in the wilderness (see Deuteronomy 8:2–3). After testing Philip by challenging him to provide the food, Jesus uses the bread and fish offered by a boy, to provide enough food for the whole crowd. Although they are well fed, the crowd are not satisfied. They want to make Jesus king. Even when Jesus removes himself by re-crossing the lake, they pursue him.

In John's account, Jesus challenges the crowd on the grounds that they only want him for the physical food that he has provided. His own temptation experience (see Matthew 4:1–4) shows that this had been a deep and challenging issue for him, and so he understands both the power of the temptation and the necessity of rooting it out.

- What do you think Jesus meant when he said, 'You must eat my flesh'?

- Why do you think this annoyed and offended some of the hearers?
- Was he deliberately being provocative, and if so, can you imagine why?
- What might it mean for us today to 'eat my flesh'? Think of ways we could convey the same meaning more clearly but with the element of provocation that the original contains.

Although many people instinctively link this passage with Communion (a subject we will explore later), what John's Gospel is underlining is that we need to absorb Jesus' teaching and lifestyle so that it becomes part of us. This is the way we will approach it now.

If you are in a group, share with one another two ways in which you see something of Jesus or his teaching in the character or behaviour of each member of the group. If saying this straight out seems scary or awkward you could write down your thoughts first. Then, when you have shared your perceptions together, you may want to talk together about views that surprised you, or reflect on how others see Jesus in you. You could conclude by praying for one another, giving thanks for the ways in which people have become like Jesus.

As a follow-up to this exercise, or as an alternative if you are reading this book on your own, why not prayerfully note down:

- two sayings of Jesus that you wish to live out more fully.
- two aspects of his character that you would like to express more regularly.
- two things you do that are unlike Jesus and that you would like to stop doing.

Then ask the Holy Spirit to help you fulfil your longings.

If you are in a group you may prefer to focus on the life of your church rather than personal issues:

- Brainstorm all the aspects of your church's life which you think embody the ways of Jesus. Make a list of the best ten.
- Brainstorm all the aspects of your church's life where you fail to live out the ways of Jesus. Pick out the most serious five.

Then decide how you can:
- celebrate the Christ-like aspects of your church.
- change the five ways in which you fail to manifest that you are the Body of Christ.

In the light of the feeding of the 5000, ask yourselves whom you could feed, and plan when to do it. After the event, read the story again and share any thoughts you have. I heard of a family in an urban priority area who had read this story together. One of the young sons then wanted to invite his friend who arrived at their door to share their pizza. As resources were scarce in this family, it was an act of considerable generosity for a hungry young man! Through this simple act, the scripture came alive to the whole family, because the boy made the connection between the heart of Jesus and his situation.

BIBLE MEDITATION

Our Bible study has shown that 'eating' in relation to God's word and Jesus' life and message implies consciously taking in the message in such a way that we fully digest it. In consequence, it becomes part of us, and we begin to express its truth in all aspects of our lives. It takes time and maybe effort (think of chewing a scroll!) to absorb the Bible. A word that conveys much the same idea is 'ruminate'. Normally that word brings to mind 'thinking about something—perhaps over a period of time'. Actually, in origin, it is another eating metaphor. 'Ruminate' is what cows do when they chew the cud and digest the results by passing it through several stomachs. We talk about 'chewing it over', too. And the word 'ruminate' is often used in connection with biblical meditation.[7]

There are several different approaches to meditation—probably the one which is currently most in vogue is the Ignatian approach, so called because it is connected with one of the great teachers of the Church, Ignatius of Loyola.[8] In its modern form, this method has a strong emphasis on entering a biblical story using our imagination, perhaps identifying with one or more of the characters in the story and seeing what God says to us in that situation. Such an approach can be very helpful. (For my application of the imagination to biblical meditation, see *God at the End of the Century* (Bible Society, 1996), pages 61–76; I also refer to other approaches to meditation and to other helpful books on pages 11–21.)

LECTIO DIVINA (DIVINE READING)

Another approach, which includes the imagination but other reflective processes too, is known as *Lectio Divina* (Divine Reading). It has a Latin name because it is an ancient way of reading the Bible, but it's one which is being rediscovered with considerable benefit to those who use it. Both the Ignatian and *Lectio Divina* methods combine deep personal (often extended) reflection and interaction with the Bible with an element of accountability to a wider group. The danger of either approach, if we do it entirely on our own, is that the Bible is dissolved in our fantasies rather than shaping our ways of seeing the world and of living in it.

Lectio Divina focuses on paying proper attention to a passage of the Bible. 'Proper attention' means recognizing that it is a sacred text—not a historical, liturgical or legal one (though, of course, different parts of the Bible can also be any one, or more, of these) but one where our primary aim is to hear what God is saying through it. The purpose of reading such a sacred text is not primarily about gaining more information but about enabling transformation, encouraging us to respond to God and to be changed through the power of his word.

This approach can be divided into four stages.

Read the words

The actual words of the text really do matter here—not just the meaning. It is a good thing to read your chosen text several times, maybe over a period of days. First read it all without stopping. Then break it up into different stages, as appropriate to the particular text, and after each stage pause and recall what you have read. It can really help to read the passage out aloud to yourself, or even use a cassette recorder and play it back to yourself. As you read it for a third time, think about any questions that come to mind. For instance, if a place is mentioned, think about where it was, what it looked like, who lived there, what was going on in it. If a person is mentioned, ask yourself what they were like, how old they were, what things mattered to them, what family they had. As you force yourself to pause like this, you will gradually deepen your familiarity with the text. Of course, you can find out answers to your questions too, from books, by asking people or by finding other references in the Bible. However, it is important to keep focused—the purpose of all of this is not to become an expert in knowledge but a child in faith, someone who is preparing to hear God through the text.

Savour the words

This stage is known as Reflecting or *Meditatio*, and is regarded as the central step. This does not mean that it is the most important, but that without it the others cannot happen. In this stage we are looking for parallels with our own lives, seeking the point where the text and our experience touch. It is where the divine message from the past can diffuse into our lives. To promote this, we need to seek consciously to be vulnerable towards God, to allow him to highlight the connections rather than forcing a link ourselves.

If the reading had been the story of the Annunciation (Luke 1:26–38), for example, those connections might appear for different people in these kinds of ways: for mothers, it might be the memory of their first awareness of being pregnant; for others, it could be receiving a message that changed their lives; for still others, it could be receiving a message that they did not fully understand at the time; it could be when we had a sense of call from God to a particular task or ministry; or when we had some kind of mystical experience. The possibilities are almost endless. What is important about this process is that, having become truly familiar with the text, a connection starts to happen because our imagination and our memories have kindled a recognition of similarity with the situation or, indeed, the meaning, of the text. Theologically it is the Holy Spirit bringing to our recollection the things concerning Christ.

At this moment of recognition (sometimes this is like a flash of lightning, startling but almost gone before we grasp it—and sometimes it is like the slow coming of the dawn—a gradual awareness that reshapes our whole outlook), the text ceases to be 'out there' and becomes part of us.

Lectio Divina *makes connections between the text and our lives; between God and us. It breaks down barriers and resistance. God never speaks to us in messages. He draws us into conversation, into dialogue with Himself through the text.*[9]

For example, the point of contact between my life and the Annunciation story was to do with receiving a message that changed my life. I remembered a phone call I received after returning home from visiting my father in hospital 20 miles away. As I entered the door, the phone rang and I picked it up, somehow knowing what the message would be. My father was dead. It meant a return journey to the hospital, but also an ongoing journey into the unknown—life without a human father—a journey which twenty years later I am spiritually still travelling as I encounter this passage in Luke's Gospel. Past and present become one reality.

'Why, Lord, why?' I question. 'Why could it not be news of life as it was for Mary? Where are you, in all of this sorrow? How will I tell my brother and sister? How will I cope with all the practical organizing that must follow this brief message?'

And as I struggle with the shock and the pain, somehow I am no longer alone—for Mary has gone this way before me, and so has the God who speaks to Mary! And through the tears and struggle which cause me emotionally to feel I am slipping into an abyss, I see the possibility of a hand-hold to save me: 'Let it be with me according to your word' (Luke 1:38, paraphrased).

So a prayer is conceived, if not yet born, in me: 'Lord, bring me to the place of surrender and acceptance, the place where Mary was.'

Feel the words

Prayer is the appropriate third stage, prayer that the word of scripture kindles, prayer that occurs as we allow the words to resonate with our experiences. It is a parallel for us with the experience of those who walked the road to Emmaus and found, although they could not say so until later, that their hearts were warmed by the companionship, rebukes and explanations of the stranger (Luke 24:13–35). That sense of warming is the kindling of prayer. Sometimes we resist it and stifle it. Sometimes it lingers within us for many days before we can fully own it as ours, either because it is a feeling we cannot express in words or because our wills are not ready to assent to its meaning. On other occasions, prayer is like a fire that ignites swiftly, releasing pent-up emotion or unresolved conflicts.

The prayer stage is very important because it is the moment when we intentionally respond to God's conversation. In the second stage ('Reflecting'), we dialogue, explore, even complain to God; or maybe we bathe or rest in the comfort of his word; or drink in, feed on, or grow by the encouragement of his word; but in prayer we concur with God in the intention of his word. Naturally the prayer need not be spoken aloud; it may be more a state of mind than any liturgical formulation, but it is a point of focus. It need not be a conclusion, rather a staging post, when we agree with God's intention and seek his help to accomplish in us what he desires as we surrender ourselves to him, even though there may be much that still resists him, doubts him or fears the future (depending on whether the passage we have been reading has been for us a probing, comforting or encouraging word). The prayer is the moment when we say with Mary, 'Behold the handmaiden of the Lord; be it unto me according to thy word' (Luke 2:38, AV).

It is no accident that in the Annunciation story the angel leaves once Mary has said these words. For this moment of prayer is the point at which the message from God becomes established firmly in our lives. The message has truly been delivered and received into our depths.

Stay in the word

The final stage is known as Resting (*Contemplatio*). It is that experience of peace, of being loved by God and of sensing that we can trust him to accomplish his purpose in us, knowing that we have given him the permission to do that. It is resting as the eagle rests in the thermal currents and so moves upwards (see Isaiah 40:31), in the moment of deep truth that God is able and we are loved by him.

Arriving at this point does not necessarily mean that we have finished with the passage. God may have many more things to say to us. What we are beginning to do through *Lectio Divina* is allowing the word to 'dwell in us richly' (Colossians 3:16, NJB), letting 'the Word of Christ in all its richness find a home with you'.

So here are a few passages to eat! Although the obvious starting point is the Gospels, I have selected four passages from Genesis and four from Acts.

Genesis 3:1–10	Acts 3:1–16
Genesis 23:1–19	Acts 6:1–10
Genesis 28:10–22	Acts 9:10–21
Genesis 45:1–15	Acts 16:6–15

- Select one passage (have a quick read of all of them and choose one that intrigues, perplexes or draws you in some way).
- Spend at least three days with this passage, reading it, and learning about the context. Find out the whole story by reading the chapters around it, discover as much as you can about the characters and situation and even the meaning of words and actions described or implied in the text. Let your mind turn to your passage when you

are waiting for a bus, or queuing in a shop, or while washing up or driving the car.

- Then choose an hour when you can be quiet and undisturbed. Now, spending 15–20 minutes, allow parallel experiences to come to mind. Write down several of these. Then select just one, or ask God to focus you on one. Writing them all down means that you can use the others another time. When you have made your choice, allow the scripture to speak into your situation—it may help to re-read the passage slowly. Alternatively, try to remember it—the advantage of this approach is that often words or situations will stick in your memory and you will begin to see the passage differently or discover another kind of response to it.
- Eventually you will be ready for the prayer stage—your intentional acknowledgment of God's word to you and your commitment to go forward with it.
- Finally, when the struggle or amazement of the prayer experience is over, rest quietly in God. You may find the following verses helpful in this final stage: they sum up what we are aspiring to.

Our Lord and our God, I turn my eyes to you, on your throne in heaven. Servants look to their masters, but we will look to you, until you have mercy on us. (Psalm 123:1–2, CEV).

I am content and at peace. As a child lies quietly in its mother's arms, so my heart is quiet within me. Israel, trust in the Lord now and for ever! (Psalm 131:2–3)

BIBLE MEALS

Meals play a very important role in the biblical story. The two best-known are the Passover and the Lord's Supper. One is particularly valued by the Jewish community and one by the Christian Church.

The basic biblical stories can be found, for the Passover, in Exodus 12:1–28 and Deuteronomy 16:3–8, and, for the Lord's Supper, in

Matthew 26:20–30; Mark 14:17–26; Luke 22:14–23; 1 Corinthians 11:23–25 (compare also John 13:1–17).

As a starting point, make a list of the similarities and differences between these meals and relate them to their present-day equivalents. The following headings will help:

- Context
- Where it first took place
- Where it normally takes place for today's believers, whether Jewish or Christian
- People involved in the story
- Who takes part today and how
- Ingredients used then and now
- What is said
- What the words recall
- What commitments follow

Moving on from this exercise, we can think about the effects of actually participating in these different meals.

A few years ago on Maundy Thursday (the day that commemorates the time when Jesus explained about his death and transformed the Passover into Communion, prior to his arrest), the church I attend arranged to have a kind of Passover meal, the *Seder*. It was not the full works, but it gave us a flavour of its significance. We sat round tables in 'family', intergenerational, groups and shared in the various parts of the meal—we lit candles, dipped parsley into salt water, symbolically washed our hands, and ate unleavened bread spread with horseradish and dipped in bitter herbs. Accompanying these symbols, we listened to the Passover readings from Exodus 3 and 12 and Psalms 113 and 114, and shared in some of the Jewish prayers that would be used at a proper Passover. I suppose it took us 30 minutes or so.

That relatively brief experience had a profound effect on me. I realized for the first time how revolutionary the Lord's Supper was. Throughout the Passover, the focus is on the events of the Exodus. The insistence on remembering is sharply fixed on what God did in that series of events and the covenant relationship that flowed from it. It is this remembering that provides the cohesion for the Jewish community, and has given hope to God's people in all kinds of desperate and frustrating situations. It was no accident that the Passover was a flashpoint for political and military revolution in Jerusalem during the Roman occupation. That was why Pilate was so keen to minimize trouble, even if it meant crucifying Jesus although he was innocent.

But why was I so impacted by this sense of revolution? I realized that Jesus had redirected all the attention from the miracle of the Exodus to himself with those simple words, 'Remember *me*'. This was a subversive and audacious challenge which I had never noticed before with anything like the same intensity. Years of theological study, including Greek and Hebrew, had failed to communicate this to me with the clarity that came from eating the meal.

Ask group members to relate their experiences of the Eucharist. Have they ever shared in a Passover-type meal? If so, how did this enrich their understanding of their faith?

Have they experienced the Eucharist in special places? Taizé? Spring Harvest? Denominational conferences? Home groups? Which do they find most helpful and why?

FURTHER AFIELD

Visit a Jewish synagogue, or arrange to meet with a local rabbi to find out about the significance of Passover for Jews. Alternatively arrange your own (simplified) Passover/*Seder*, along these lines.

You will need:
- candles to light
- a bowl of water for hand-washing
- some *matzah* (unleavened bread—you can always bake your own)
- the shank bone of a lamb
- bitter herbs (normally horseradish leaf, lettuce or even dandelion leaves)

- a bowl of *haroshet* to represent the mud the Israelites needed for making bricks in Egypt (cooked apple, with chopped nuts and fragments of cinnamon stick to represent the straw that they also needed. The mixture can be thinned down with honey)
- parsley (to dip in the salt water)
- a hardboiled egg (which is a symbol of mourning for the Jews)
- salt water (representing the tears of slavery)
- a tray on which to place the six food items listed immediately above
- a glass or glasses, plus wine

In a full service there are four times when wine is drunk, corresponding to the four promises in Exodus 6:6–7: 'I will bring you out'; 'I will deliver you (from slavery)'; 'I will redeem you'; 'I will take you for my people'.

The basic order of the service is as follows:

- Candles are lit by the host(ess).
- The first cup of wine is drunk.
- The leader washes his/her hands.
- Parsley is dipped in salt water and all eat it.
- Some unleavened bread is broken in two (the smaller piece is hidden for the children to find at the end—a small prize is given).
- The tray on which the six elements have been placed is raised and then there are several readings—which could be read to accompany the appropriate elements in the meal or as a continuous set, using different readers or with all reading together. The readings are Deuteronomy 6:20–25 or Exodus 12:25–26 (perhaps ask a younger person to read this), Exodus 12:1–13 and Exodus 12:21–23. The lamb bone can be raised by the leader at the references to the Passover lamb.
- Psalms 113 and 114 are read out (or sung).
- Everyone drinks wine.
- Everyone washes their hands.
- The unleavened bread is shared out and all eat.
- People eat the bitter herbs (dip the lettuce leaf in the *horeshet* and make a small sandwich with two pieces of *matzah*).
- The leader offers a prayer of thanks to God for his goodness.

- The third cup of wine is drunk.
- Psalms 115—118 (in whole or part) are read out.
- The leader offers prayers of praise.
- The fourth cup of wine is drunk (traditionally known as 'Elijah's cup', as his return was expected to precede the Messiah's coming).
- Final blessing.

There are, of course, many more details in a full *Seder*, including several special prayers and blessings. The Church's Ministry among the Jews have some helpful resources—see Resources section for the address.

As a group, attend other kinds of 'communion' services from Roman Catholic Mass to Brethren 'breaking of bread', remembering to respect both their and your church's guidelines on how far you can participate. Or just go to your favourite restaurant, together, and thank God for the occasion.

PRAYER

Lord God, people need food—we remember before you all those near and far away who have worked hard to ensure that we have enough to eat today.

People enjoy food—we remember with gratitude those very special meals, with trusted friends, on festive occasions, at times of celebration.

People need more than food—we remember before you all those who have made the Bible enticing for us, through the fragrance of their lives and through the attraction of their words.

People enjoy more than food—we remember with gratitude those very special times when, in casual moments or intentional listening, we have sensed your words for us.

Please continue to sustain us with your truths and help us to share your story with others so that they too can be nourished for their journeys. We ask this through Jesus Christ our Lord. Amen.

Chapter 5

TWIST IT

ICE-BREAKERS

1. What's your favourite story of all time (excluding anything from the Bible)? It can be a real-life story, even autobiographical, or it can be fiction, from fairy stories, through Rosamunde Pilcher to Albert Camus. You can even use an incident from a soap opera. Write down no more than five main components of this story on (at the most) one side of A4 paper. Why do you really like this story? Is it the suspense, the twist in the tail, the characters, the message or what? If you are in a group, share your stories in threes or fours.

2. Think of a joke you like or have heard recently that made you laugh. Tell these jokes to each other. What makes them 'good jokes'? Is it the sudden change of perspective or perception, the meaning of the words, the way you visualize the scene, or the outcomes?

3. Put up a chart of ten current soap operas (radio can be included as well as TV). Then invite people to note down their three favourites. Collate the results and discuss what makes the favourite ones so popular.

    An alternative here is to stage a mini-debate. Decide on three top soaps. TV magnates are going to chop two of them, and people have to choose which one they want to see preserved. They then get into groups and take five minutes to come up with ideas as to why their favourite should be kept. Next, each group appoints a spokesperson, who has two minutes to persuade the TV magnates that their choice is best.

INTRODUCTION

A deceptively simple way to enjoy the Bible and to enthuse others about it is to turn it back into story, or release the story from the printed page. This can take many forms and be used in many contexts, as we shall see. But first it is important to recognize how central story is for the Bible itself.

The Bible can be viewed as a large-scale story with, of course, hundreds of smaller stories within it. Because there is such a rich variety of different styles and types, different cultural contexts and characters, it is easy to forget that the real subject of the story is God and his dealings with human beings.

When we say 'Bible' we think instinctively of a printed book, but for most of its lifespan most people have encountered the Bible as visual or audible story. Of course, when we use the word 'story' about the Bible, we are not implying that it is untrue, rather the opposite—that it is so richly true that only a story will do to convey that truth. Stories are meant to be told! The supreme example is Jesus—the Word made flesh. Rather than giving us a comprehensive, analytical treatise about himself, God gave us the story of a human life. We need to approach many parts of the Bible with a story-focused head and heart rather than an analytical mind. Reducing every biblical account to three points beginning with 'p' (for example) may sound neat and tidy, but it can end up being more like a skeleton of the message rather than the living reality.

BIBLE STUDY

Here are some examples to illustrate the importance of story in the Bible and therefore for us as we encounter the Bible.

DEUTERONOMY 6:20–25

This passage encourages Israel to answer their children's enquiries about why they should obey God's laws, in terms of their deliverance from Egypt and the blessings which will come to the nation if they faithfully observe God's directions. It shows us several important things about story.

- Within the Bible, God's laws, in terms of both their giving and their obeying, make sense only in the context of a story. If we approach these laws from our experience and understanding of 'law', then we will misunderstand their purpose. From our experience the law can appear as something that catches us out, like a speed camera, or something that lawyers wrangle over. The Gospels show us that the 'teachers of the law' in the time of Jesus had developed similar attitudes. Within the Old Testament, however, the laws are presented as a gracious gift of God to help his people as they move through their history; often, too, they are 'given' in a context of worship, so they are understood as an important aspect of God's relationship with his people.
- Many stories answer (or investigate) questions. Sometimes there is an explicit question, as in Deuteronomy 6:20. On other occasions, as with the story of the tower of Babel (Genesis 11), it is a hidden question: 'How does it come about that there are so many languages?' (see v. 9). It is usually illuminating to discover which type of questions the story is dealing with.
- Stories are told in a context. This one in Deuteronomy was a family context, probably to do with celebrating the Passover. But stories make fuller sense when they are told in a context of trust and respect, and that is one reason why, if we share our testimony with friends, it can have a more powerful impact than when we share it with strangers.
- In Exodus 12:26–27, there is a passage with a similar structure, but this time it explains why the Israelites were keeping the Passover. This reminds us that central to the Church's liturgies is the telling of a

story, in the context of Holy Communion, the meal that established the new covenant (see Matthew 26:17–30; 1 Corinthians 11:17–33).

LUKE 4:14–30

This passage relates the visit of Jesus to his own synagogue in Nazareth, as he is beginning his public ministry. He is invited to read the scriptures; the passage is from Isaiah 61, explaining how the 'anointed one' will help the weak and disadvantaged. Jesus claims that he is fulfilling these verses. The immediate response of his listeners is that of amazement and praise. But it doesn't end there!

This incident is full of important insights and provocations, but we are concentrating here only on one matter. Why did the congregation, which was initially full of praise for Jesus, end up attempting to murder him?

The turning point is in the two stories Jesus told (vv. 25–27). Of course, we only have the punch-lines from these stories and we need to understand the context if we are to make sense of the plot.

The stories about Elijah and Elisha were great resources for those who felt they were oppressed by a foreign power, as most Jews did at the time of Jesus. For they were all about God cleansing the nation of foreign influences and removing foreign oppressors. What is more, they showed the prophets outwitting those who had compromised by becoming involved with foreign powers or worshipping foreign gods. The stories taught people to be zealous for Yahweh and his people and not to rely on human resources alone. God was a God who was able to intervene in amazing ways. Such wonderful, heroic stories fuelled Jewish faith and nationalism.

The meaning that Jesus drew from these icons of nationalism, however, was that God was as committed to the Gentiles as he was to the Jews. That was where the cutting challenge of Jesus hit home hardest. It had been there in his failure to quote the last line of the passage from Isaiah 61, which spoke about God wreaking revenge on his enemies. His audience either missed that or gave Jesus the benefit of the doubt. But when he took their own favourite national heroes and turned the message of their stories on its head, they could not resist picking up the gauntlet Jesus had thrown down. Retelling their stories was more than they could stand—and that is why they tried to kill him. Such is the power of story.

LUKE 24:13–35

Here is another powerful biblical affirmation of the power of storytelling.

Luke's account of the two on the road to Emmaus is so simple, memorable and evocative that it would probably do well if it were entered in a competition for the world's best-ever short story. But the point we will focus on is how the story of the death and resurrection of Jesus is told and retold here.

There are, I think, four different ways in which this story is told within the Emmaus narrative. Can you spot all four?

1. Cleopas and his friend are reliving the story of the terrible things that had happened to Jesus as they make their mournful and probably fearful journey home (v. 14).

2. They tell the story to Jesus in response to his question, 'What things?' (v. 19). Probably this was a very similar account to the one that they were sharing between themselves as they journeyed, before Jesus joined them. It was a desperately sad story, of the victory of economic, political and military power over God's purposes, the dissolution of fundamental hopes and the confusion of reality by some bemused women.

3. Jesus tells the story from the perspective of the Old Testament (see vv. 25–27). Now it is a story set in a much bigger context—the whole sweep of God's plan as revealed through the prophets. Illuminated with the lamp of this divine history, the story sounds very different. All that had happened was within God's plan (that is the meaning of 'Was it not necessary...?' See v. 26 and compare 9:22, 'must suffer'). This time the story ends not with the victory of powerful men, nor with the supposed imaginings of a bunch of women, but with the Messiah entering his glory!

4. The final version is by the original storytellers, but we can imagine how different it is now (see vv. 33–35). They have hurried back the dozen miles to Jerusalem, in spite of the very real dangers to their own lives both during the journey in the dark and on their entry into Jerusalem. They should be exhausted but they are totally energized by their meeting with the risen Lord, and the whole experience, including their account of Jesus' death, bubbles out again. Once again the emotional and mental state of the storytellers, as well as the relationship between the tellers and hearers, radically changes the significance of the story.

If your group is large enough, divide into three groups, each focusing on a different version—2, 3 or 4. Work out how you think your particular story would have sounded and then, when you have finished, listen to one another's accounts. Here are a few questions to bear in mind:

- How similar and how different are the stories in terms of characters, plot, mood?
- Why are they different? To what extent do they now reflect the perspective of the original storytellers—Cleopas or Jesus? To what extent do they reflect the personalities of the people in the group who put the story together?
- Are all the versions 'true'? If so, what makes them true? Is it the facts that are mentioned, or that they were true from the perspective of the teller, or that they convey something true—for instance, about the nature of Jesus and the resurrection, or even about being human?

STORYTELLING AND TRUTH

In the Bible studies, we have seen not only how fundamental story is to the Bible. We have also seen that different accounts can all be true, from the perspective of the characters. In the Emmaus story from Luke, the same events (Jesus' death and resurrection) can be communicating very different messages according to the context in which the story is set and the emotional perspective of the teller. Then when these accounts are set within their own story (the journeys to and from Emmaus), they communicate even more effectively.

Storytelling is both flexible and powerful. Think, for instance, how the small number of basic stories around the birth of Jesus have been retold in multiple ways through the centuries, in painting, music, stained glass, Christmas cards, nativity plays and carols.

But such a wide range of retelling or representation raises some important questions about the 'truth' of these accounts. When a medieval artist depicts the nativity scene with a shed and people dressed in medieval clothes, rather than an authentic Near Eastern scene, has he disowned or at least distorted truth, or has he communicated the reality as effectively as possible to his own viewers?

If we return to Luke's Gospel, we can see that he tells many other stories of a quite different kind, which also raise questions about truth. For Luke, like Matthew and Mark, tells the stories that Jesus told—his parables. One of the best-known, poignant and powerful of these is the one we know as the 'prodigal son' (Luke 15:11–32). It could just as well be called the story of the 'waiting father' or the 'older brother'. How people perceive it affects profoundly the way it is told, and often the telling stops with the return of the prodigal, which is rather like ending the Emmaus story with the arrival in the village! You could share your recollections of the way this story has been told and used in sermons and see whether you think the accounts you have heard were true to the whole of the story.

However, there is another aspect to the issues of truth and story. Is the 'story of the prodigal son' true? If you are puzzled about how to answer that question, you are in good company. If we mean 'Did it happen as history?', then the answer would be 'No', but that doesn't mean it is not true. Its truth is determined not by its 'historicity' but by its impact on our human lives. Somehow the story moves us and carries us along. And the life, death and resurrection of Jesus justify the story; they demonstrate that the story is valid, because it shows us what God is like—he is a forgiving father, as countless returning prodigals have found. So it is a story which has, in this sense, happened many times in history! So the 'story of the prodigal son' is true, even if it is not an event that actually happened once, in a specific place.

Indeed, because it has 'happened' many times, there is a way in which the story is more true than if it was only a historical event with no personal application. Often, preachers who deal with this parable, or indeed any parable, will attempt to say '…and this is what it means'. It may appear to be a simple story which can be transferred into logical propositions, but two things at least should make us question this. The first is that Jesus said that parables were comprehensible only to those who understood the secret of the Kingdom. The second is that whole books have been written to explain its meaning, and even so there is always something left over. This parable, as with many good stories, is richer than any statements we can make about it. The truth is fuller than statement. Just as music can be described in words but such a description is not the same as listening to the music, so with parable and story, including storytelling of biblical events: any explanation is less than the experience of hearing the story told. That is one reason why Christians do well to relearn the art of telling stories from the Bible. After all, much of the Bible was transmitted orally before it was written down.

SHARING STORIES

Here are some ways to learn some of the skills that make a good storyteller. These suggestions are meant for small groups because we can learn both by doing and by observing others.

DESERT ISLAND

Imagine that you are marooned on a desert island with two other people. You all speak the same language but apart from that you do not know anything about one another. You have three minutes each to tell the others a story from your own life which will best help them to understand the kind of person you are.

Spend a few minutes thinking about an event in your life that encapsulates some important things about yourself. Next, jot down a few points to help you share this briefly.

Now, in groups of three on your 'desert island', tell your stories, one at a time, with the other two listening. If you are a listener, write down up to four things that this story tells you about the storyteller. Finally, check your points with the teller. Are they surprised at your insight?

Repeat this for all three people in your group.

BALLOON DEBATE

You are in a hot-air balloon. Unfortunately, as you fly over the mountains, a mountain peak just punctures the balloon, so you are losing altitude. Every few minutes someone has to be thrown overboard, or all lives will be lost. The group decide that they will tell stories to decide who stays in and who is thrown out. They can be funny stories, horror stories or personal experiences.

Think of a story that you really like and think will appeal to the others, and decide how you can tell it in two minutes.

At the end, when you have heard everyone's story, you each have three votes to cast for your favourite stories. The person with the least number of votes is 'thrown out'—or if you are feeling kind, sent to make the coffee!

A GOOD STORY

Presumably the best story won and its teller was the last to survive!

So what exactly is a 'good story'? There are several possibilities:

- If a child is trying to explain how they have come to have a packet of chewing-gum in their pocket when they are not allowed to do so, if we say, 'Um, that's a good story', we mean, 'Well, I suppose you think that's plausible enough to be convincing; I agree it's a good try but still laughable!'

- A good story could be one that encourages 'good', that is, morally positive, behaviour.
- The term could also describe an 'appropriate' story, illustrating a particular point in a presentation or sermon, for instance. It could also mean that the story was wisely selected to engage a particular audience, or even that it was effective because it was memorable.
- The word 'good' could be used in an aesthetic sense, describing a pleasing, imaginative, coherent, believable story with sharp and engaging characterization.

Mention to one another (if you are in a group) or write down (if you are on your own) about six examples of what you consider to be a good story from the Bible. Then consider which of the meanings of 'good' above apply to your choice. Expect to find that more than one type of 'good' applies to each story.

The value of this exercise is that it helps us to identify the different meanings of a 'good' story and how they intertwine.

WHY RETELL THE BIBLE?

By now, you should all be on the way to becoming excellent storytellers! But why should we retell the Bible? Are the Gospels, for instance, not good enough as they stand? Indeed, if we rework Bible stories do we not run the risk of distorting the truth?

Certainly, as with preaching which is based on a passage of the Bible, it is possible to distort a story or apply it inappropriately. That is one reason why it is good to belong to a storytelling group, so that personal biases can be spotted and corrected. But there are advantages in retelling the stories. For instance, through the use of dialects or characterization, it is possible to give biblical stories a more direct impact for people. The effect can be similar to that experienced by people who hear some part of the Bible in their own language for the first time: it speaks to the heart and mind with greater directness and often leads to a more potent response. People can be engaged with the story before they spot that it is 'from the Bible'. An illustration of this is the story that Nathan, the prophet, told King David about the rich man stealing the poor man's pet lamb—thus trapping David into confessing his own guilt (2 Samuel 12:1–13).

Another advantage is that the story can be told from a different perspective to that of the biblical narrative. This brings a fresh encounter for the hearers, and can be especially valuable with well-known stories where familiarity can breed boredom. One great way to alleviate boredom is to retell the story by setting it in a totally different context. Below is an illustration of this approach. Read it to yourself or, if you are in a group, arrange for one member to read it aloud and the others to listen. Make a note of the point in the story when you recognize which biblical narrative it is retelling.

A REAL DEAL

We were on our way to Edinburgh. It was one of those short city-breaks—an amazing bargain, especially when you consider it was the Easter weekend. But for us it was a chore, not an adventure or delight. Even as we made our way from the airport lounge to the plane, each of us wished we had the courage to turn back, but we didn't. We carried on, because we both realized that it was probably our last chance, yet we both knew that there wasn't much of a hope.

Our trouble was that we were struggling with bereavement—an utterly tragic and terrible death. It had shattered our lives. Death with no end; death that breeds inside you.

He was our very best friend, although we hadn't known him for that long. We had first met him, ironically it now seemed, at a wedding. Losing him, we both felt, was worse than losing your partner or your President. When you were with him, you knew that there must be answers to every problem in the world, however catastrophic, but you also knew that your own problems were in safe hands too. Confidence and peace flowed out of him and warmed you like sunshine. True, we didn't always understand exactly what he was saying, but there was no doubt that it made sense and seemed to get things sorted.

Yet such insight was only a part of him. He had presence—what you might call 'royal presence'—and poise. He did things to change situations —defused violence, saved marriages, restored sanity and always kept the party going. Some of our friends said he had sorted out health problems too. Kindness, generosity, security, fairness... the list could go on, but no amount of words begins to colour in his picture. Everyone who met him loved him with more love than they even knew they had—or so we felt. How wrong we had been.

There were people, it seems—powerful people, proud people—who were deeply troubled by him. The press corps started to pursue him. It probably didn't help that he could always turn the tables with his penetrating responses. Like the time the journalist from *The Tabloid* tried to get him to condemn the Secretary of State for the affairs she was reputedly involved in. 'You tell me what your wife thinks of your sexual experiments with boys when you were in Thailand three weeks ago, and I'll tell you what I think of the Secretary of State.' The journalist tried to dissolve into the crowd of reporters, but everyone got edgy. You could sense the worry rippling through them: 'If he knows that, what does he know about me?'

Then eight days later, it happened. The police said that it looked like a gangland killing. His body had been brutalized, then burnt. There was not enough of him left for a decent burial, just enough for us to know his end had been utterly ghastly. Whatever the truth, we felt destroyed too, but we couldn't die. Our pain was being turned, like a blowtorch, on each other. This Easter break was our last attempt to hang on to our marriage.

Somehow we got to our hotel. I suppose it was OK and deserved its four stars, but we didn't really care. We settled in, with yet another acid row followed by a black silence. At last we went down to dinner. Why, I don't know, unless it was the thing to do. We certainly weren't hungry. Maybe we thought we would be forced to be civil, with other people around us. But what we hadn't planned for was that they would sit anyone else at our table. He was a man on his own—just what we didn't want, and our looks told the waitress that. He must have seen our horrified look too, but he sat down anyway. Basically we ignored him. We didn't go through the normal pleasantries, we didn't even look at him.

Even so, after a few minutes he broke the silence. In spite of the frigid tension between us, his voice was relaxed and warming. Gently, he walked into our dark pain. Strangely, he didn't seem to know about the terrible tragedy, even though our dead friend's picture had been splashed all over the papers. In this stranger's company we began to spill it all out, not only the facts but our deepest feelings of hopelessness and despair. Yet, he took our anguish and wrapped it in another story of another good and compassionate person, whose friends had felt the same as we did, only worse, if possible. He too had been done to death, but from him had burst an unstoppable flowering of life, love, caring service, hope, community and courage. 'This is the way the story at the heart of the universe must unfold,' he said. 'I thought your friend had told you so. Would you like some salad?'

As he spoke those last few words, we both looked up towards one another and knew. We knew that the impossible was true. This man at our table was our dearest friend, our hope and our life.

After listening to this story, discuss together to what extent it is right to adapt stories when they are historically based, as this one is. Or is such large-scale adaptation only appropriate for accounts which are clearly 'stories' within the text—parables are an obvious example.

Choose a Bible account of an event (here are a few suggestions: Genesis 44; Exodus 3; Joshua 2; Judges 7; 2 Samuel 7; 1 Kings 21; Nehemiah 2; Matthew 2:19–23; Mark 3:1–6; Luke 10:38–42; John 7:37–44), or a parable, and transpose it into your cultural setting. Either work on this as a group or on your own. First think through the story from the particular perspective of one character, rather than, as is normally the case with biblical narratives, that of a reporter or observer. Then think of possible parallels in our world. Do not strive to get every detail transposed, but at least seek to bring out the main point(s) of the story. For instance, could the Gideon story (Judges 7) be transposed to a modern inner-city area where a boy is hiding from a gang and the police come along and choose him to be the community representative? What about placing Elijah's confrontation with Ahab over Naboth's vineyard (1 Kings 21) in a garage that restores classic cars?

Naboth's vineyard could become a Rolls-Royce Silver Ghost and so on. Once you have imaginatively reworked the story, it is interesting to reflect on any new insights that emerge, as well as keeping a check on what has become lost in the process.

Why not share your stories and write them up for a church newsletter, or arrange an evening where stories, including yours, are told, maybe accompanied by cheese and wine.

REMEMBERING THE STORY

At the other end of the spectrum, storytelling can be a straight retelling of the biblical text, reciting it from memory. There are many techniques to help with this process of memorization. Some people find it useful to tape-record the story and play it back to themselves repeatedly. Others prefer to divide the biblical passage into different scenes and imagine them; then take each scene and learn the words that belong there, picturing the whole process. Others find it easier to learn in a group, starting by reading the passage to one another, and gradually becoming less reliant on the text. Then they can retell it without even holding the text but with the comfort that someone else will prompt them if they forget. Some people find they learn a story best by writing it out and saying it to themselves as they write. Others, with good verbal memories, simply get on and learn it!

At first glance this raises the question 'Why bother?' Why not simply read from the Bible and gain 100 per cent accuracy? Now while a good reader can engage us and communicate effectively, storytelling does more.

Storytelling involves eye contact and body language. It provides you as the 'speaker' with the freedom to move and to develop a more dynamic relationship with the audience. So, if you sense that you are losing your audience's interest, you can use a variety of approaches to regain it:

- Shout louder.
- Speak faster.
- Speak slower.

- Go silent.
- Move closer to a member of the audience who is clearly not engaged.
- Turn your back on the audience.

If you are in a group, (a) share which of these techniques you favour; and (b) try some out, with one person telling a familiar story and others acting bored!

This kind of storytelling is not simply about memory and technique, however. It is also about engagement with the text. We want the audience to be impacted by the text as we tell the story, not primarily thinking about what wonderful memories we have! We want them to hear it more clearly than ever before, so that God can speak into their lives and call them to some kind of response. And if we want this for others, then we must be prepared to allow it to happen to us as well.

Again, there are a number of approaches to engaging with the text, some of which will be more helpful to one person and some to another. It is also true that different approaches work better with different kinds of material. So, here are a few—but please feel free to develop and discover your own.

- Read the passage several times over a number of days.
- Prayerfully ask God what he wants to say to you and others through this passage.
- Spend time imagining what it was like to be different characters in the story.
- Seek to understand what God was saying to the different characters and how he was working in their lives.
- Work out the overall purpose or message of the passage and how best to communicate it.

When you sense you know what the message of the passage is, then spend time working out how to tell it so that the message becomes clearer through the telling. Think about the speed of your delivery, the level of sound (do you shout or whisper?), what kind of accents to use, whether dramatic gestures will underline the key words, how to use silence, whether you approach the audience at any point, whether you take up different positions for different speakers, and so on.

If you want to analyse some of these techniques, the video *Tales from the Madhouse* (available from Bible Society) shows many of them in action. *Tales from the Madhouse* is a retelling of people's encounters with Jesus—all the characters having been in some way involved in the events surrounding his death. The setting, however, is not a biblical one, but all the characters are residents of a Victorian asylum—hence the title.

USING STORYTELLING

WHEN

There are two distinct contexts for storytelling—formal and informal.

A formal context includes using story as part of a wider message—alongside (before or after) or even within a sermon, for example, which can be very effective. Please remember that storytelling can work well with children and young people too (we have been emphasizing its adult use), so it could be the centrepiece for an all-age service, or it could be used at a youth group weekend instead of a straightforward devotional item.

Formal contexts also include events which are primarily about storytelling. So, if your church is involved in the town's carnival or some other kind of festival, why not set up a storytelling centre, where refreshments are available free?

Many libraries have storytelling times and events: these could provide an excellent context for us to tell our stories in the wider world. So, once you have developed your skills, and perhaps gained some accreditation through The Telling Place, for instance (see Resources section), approach your local library and offer your services. It would probably be good to mix biblical stories with others in this context.

Storytelling can also be used in the context of a school or toddler group, where the main purpose is, say, to help parents (and grand-parents, uncles and aunts) become better storytellers to their children.

In that process, biblical stories can be told imaginatively to introduce people to the vast riches that are there.

Storytelling in assemblies or as part of Religious Education or English lessons provides other formal opportunities.

Storytelling therefore provides us with opportunities for 'breaking out and breaking in' with the good news of God. In these kinds of context, it is the process of storytelling that provides the access, so it is important that the quality of both the stories and the retelling is good. Then, from the audience's viewpoint, what the story is or where it comes from is secondary and should mean that biblical stories are as acceptable as any others.

Informal contexts can be anything from the bus queue to the pub or coffee shop, the home to the workplace. The stories we tell can be a rehash of what we saw on TV or the cinema, something we read in the paper or heard in the street, anything that has happened to us. If we become known as a good, fascinating, humorous, short (and here it can hardly be too emphatic!) storyteller, people will start to look to us as a source of entertainment and wisdom. Then, it may become appropriate to throw in the occasional biblical story too. Perhaps a good way to start this is to say, 'I heard a great story the other day. would you like to hear it?' or, 'That's an interesting/difficult issue— I heard a story that might help us…'.

WHERE

Here are some ways to use storytelling in your church:

- Offer to tell a story as part of the application of the Bible reading in a church service. Obviously this needs to be worked out carefully with the preacher and the church's leadership. Having done this, invite others to join you in a group if they are interested in discovering more about storytelling.
- Write a brief story for your church newsletter and then invite people along to a exploratory meeting, where you could work through this chapter together.

- Invite a good storyteller to speak at a normal church event, such as a women's meeting, men's breakfast or whatever, and then be ready to pick up on the interest generated. (The Northumbria Community, who run The Telling Place, will probably be able to recommend one who does not live too far from you—see the Resources section for contact details.)
- You could use a tape of someone telling biblical stories, to fuel interest.
- Organize a storytelling festival. Many of the practical issues mentioned in the 'flower festival' section (see pages 49–54) about time and place will have relevance here. However, there are some special points to bear in mind. The atmosphere for storytelling is important, so think about which room you will use and how you will 'dress' it to create a relaxed and expectant audience. To generate a sense of community, it may be helpful to begin with a meal. Then you need to decide whether you will bring in professional story-tellers or do it yourselves. Are you going to have a theme for the stories, tell all the stories from one biblical book or have a random mixture? Will you use one style of storytelling or will you offer a variety? Is your intended audience mainly church people or are you wanting to engage people who do not normally read or hear the Bible. Then, having sorted all this out, you will need to think about how to promote the event and how to get it reported in the local press so that the Bible is given a positive image through your storytelling.

Storytelling is a powerful means of communication today—it is warm and richly human, it echoes the past and yet fits in the present. Among our image-saturated, media-dominated lives, its simplicity penetrates our sophistication and stays to help, comfort and provoke. Learning to be a 'biblical' storyteller will change your life and the lives of those who listen to you.

FURTHER AFIELD

Find out about storytelling events in your area: the Northumbria Community may be able to supply information. It might be interesting to visit a secular and a Christian event and compare them.

PRAYER

Eternal God, you chose to reveal yourself most perfectly through the story of one human life, your son and our saviour—Jesus.

Help us to be so at home in the worlds and words of the Bible that we can reimagine the meaning of his story for our times.

Help us to know the Bible's characters, to walk its ways and to respond to the music of its words so deeply that we can breathe its life through the stories we tell.

Help us to absorb its wisdom and its values so fully that we become its storytellers in all that we are as well as all that we say, so that you can reveal yourself again through the imperfect lives we offer to you.

We ask this through your Son and our Saviour—Jesus Christ. Amen.

Chapter 6

PRAY IT

ICE-BREAKERS

1. Invite people to bring their favourite prayer to the next session and share them at the start of the meeting. (Encourage people to choose short ones.)
2. What was your most 'emergency' prayer for help? (For example, mine was when I thought I was going to be cut in half by an articulated lorry that swung out from a 'T' junction straight across the path of my car.)
3. Work out in pairs what you think Noah might have prayed as the door was shut on the Ark (Genesis 7:1–16), what Daniel might have prayed when he was thrown into the lions' den (Daniel 6:11–17), or Jesus when the disciples were still disputing who was the greatest, at the Last Supper (Luke 22:24–30). Then read your prayers to one another.
4. Did your parents (or someone similar, like your grandma) teach you a prayer as a child, perhaps at bedtime? Share your recollections.

INTRODUCTION

As we realized in the last chapter, the Bible is often considered as God's story, telling of God's relationship with the whole human race from the beginning to the end. There are valid reasons for looking at it this way. But alongside that, we could also say that the Bible is the story of prayer. If we think about prayer as our conversations with God, then the Bible is a rich hoard of treasures. We could describe it as a museum with prayer 'artefacts' on display for us, but a museum suggests things to look at and wonder about, rather than something we can actually use, whereas the prayers in the Bible can be used in all kinds of ways.

Which metaphor would you choose to describe to other people the way in which the Bible helps you in your praying?

If you are with a group, take a minute on your own to jot down two pictures that come to mind. (Please do not reject your pictures if initially they strike you as odd. Sometimes they spring into our minds and we have to work out why they are appropriate.) Then, share your pictures or metaphors. Don't worry if you can't explain them exactly— perhaps someone else will illuminate the significance for you. Finally, select three pictures that you find insightful. They may include your own or you may want to drop yours and pick up other people's. If someone in the group is artistic, then why not record your insights visually?

We mentioned earlier that prayer is an integral part of the Bible's story. So we are now going to look at a couple of examples of this— one from the beginning and one from the end of the Bible.

BIBLE STUDY

GENESIS 3:8–13

This is a wonderfully perceptive and sensitive story which has at its heart a conversation between God and Adam. Of course, it is not prayer if by prayer we mean only 'asking God for things'—Adam asks for nothing. It is prayer, however, at a more profound level, for it is a person answering to the call of God. Often we think that prayer is us calling to God, but the reality is depicted here for us. God asks, 'Where are you?' This enquiry makes prayer a possibility. God is looking and longing for us; he is also listening to what we say, as the verses go on to make clear. This story provides us with another insight about prayer: it should be a time when we listen to God and he searches our hearts. This is the risk in real prayer: through it we stretch out to touch the heart of God, but as we do, he can touch our hearts, to rebuke or challenge, direct or enrich. But this prayer conversation sets the scene for the rest of human history. There are many more insights in this passage about the nature of prayer. Here are a few more:

- Prayer is intensely personal, but inevitably others are drawn into our conversation with God.
- Prayer can result in significant outcomes, even when there are no direct requests (see vv. 14–19).
- Prayer is about establishing the justice of God in our world. God brings Adam and Eve to an open realization of what they have done before pronouncing his actions, which establish that the words of the serpent about God are false.

REVELATION 22:17-21

Here, as we approach the very end of God's story as set out within the pages of the Bible, is another passage with many valuable clues about prayer. The Spirit is, of course, the Holy Spirit who communicates the mind of God to us but who also helps us in our praying. The Bride is the whole Church of Jesus Christ. Prayer is at its best, both in terms of the depth of the experience for us and in terms of the impact on others and the world, when the Spirit and the Bride speak in unison. Here, in one and the same breath, God's will is revealed (by the Spirit to the Church) and affirmed (by the Church to the Spirit): the Spirit and the Bride say, 'Come!' (v. 17). When this happens, we are praying, 'Your kingdom come, your will be done on earth as in heaven.' We are not praying alone, carrying out our spiritual warfare like isolated soldiers, but empowered by the Spirit we fight together.

If we read verse 17, we might well wonder whether 'Come!' is a prayer at all. Initially it seems to be an invitation for people to respond to the gospel. To understand the content of this prayer, we need to look back to verse 12, where Jesus says, 'I am coming soon!', and then on to verse 20. Now it is clear that the prayer is to Jesus to come and roll up the carpet of history. Here again we can learn something of the heart of prayer. If Jesus has announced that he is coming soon, why do we need to pray for it? In the mystery of God, his plans are not fulfilled without our affirmation and participation. One of the many wonders of prayer that humble and exalt me at the same time is that God chooses to wait for us to ask before he moves, even in response to his own promises. This is why God's story and the prayers of the Bible go hand in hand. To pray the Bible, then, is to read it properly.

THE PRAYERS OF JESUS

Other parts of the Bible that relate prayer to the unfolding story are the Gospel accounts of Jesus. Again they show deep understanding of the reality of prayer, and we see this nowhere more so than in Jesus' prayers from the cross.

These prayers of Jesus have been subject to detailed analysis and have provided endless meditations—and with good reason. For here we see prayer at its most extreme—an intense situation of need but also potential accomplishment; a place of violent testing but, because it is Jesus praying, of profound revelation about the nature of prayer. What emerges in Mark 15:34 is that in these very conditions Jesus 'prays the Bible': 'Jesus shouted, "*Eloi, Eloi, lema sabachthani*?" which means, "My God, my God, why have you deserted me?"' (CEV).

Strange as it may seem at first, these shocking words, known as 'the cry of dereliction', are a quotation from the Old Testament. They come from the beginning of Psalm 22, a very poignant and powerful psalm. Jesus may have been using this quotation alone to express his situation as it was, or he may have run through the whole psalm in his mind. Read Psalm 22 now and note down some of its content:

- How the psalmist feels about God, particularly his relationship with God.
- What the psalmist affirms about God.

- What the psalmist asks for from God.
- What the future expectation of the psalmist is.

What difference does this knowledge make to our understanding of the mind of Jesus?

It is worth noting that the quotation is not in the formal Hebrew of the scriptures as they would have been read in the synagogue, but in Aramaic, the popular language actually used by Jewish people in the time of Jesus. If you want a parallel, Jesus was not quoting the Authorized Version or even the New English Bible but the Good News Bible or even J.B. Phillips.

The most important point is that we get a glimpse here of the value of using scripture in prayer; probably Jesus had used these words many times before and, in his own desperate situation, they were available to help him sustain his relationship with God.

Having looked at some of the insights the Bible provides about prayer, it is now time for us to become more active in using the Bible to shape and resource our own praying.

WAYS TO PRAY THE BIBLE

REPETITION (BUT NOT 'VAIN')

The most obvious way to pray the Bible is to repeat some of its prayers. The Church has done this throughout time. Perhaps the best-known are the Magnificat (Luke 1:46–55), the Benedictus (Luke 2:29–33) and, in the Eastern Church especially, the Jesus Prayer: 'Lord Jesus Christ, Son of God, have mercy on me, a sinner'. If you look carefully at the Magnificat, you might wonder whether it is a prayer at all. Apparently it is not addressed to God: he is referred to not in the second person (you) but in the third person (he). There are two reasons why this can count as a prayer, however. First, it is a confession of faith in God and a preparation for meeting God. As such it is the expression of a person who is in communion with God—and this is prayer. Second, grammar can be deceptive—sometimes when we are expressing the deep things within us, we are really looking Godward, so using the third person grammatically is a kind of cover for talking to God, a way of opening ourselves to God and inviting him to listen in. I don't think God is too bothered about the right grammar!

Probably the most universally repeated biblical prayer is 'The Lord's Prayer'.[10] This can be found in two places in the Gospels—Matthew 6:9–13 and Luke 11:2–4 (a shorter version). There are good reasons why this prayer is so well used. First, it is a prayer that comes from Jesus himself; second, it is presented in both Gospels as a kind of model prayer for disciples; and third, it is a brilliant pattern to follow. Using the wording in Matthew (from the Authorized Version), let's look at it phrase by phrase, thinking about ways in which this prayer can be used to shape our own praying.

'Our Father'

How we approach and address God is very significant. Inevitably any address can become an empty ritual, something we say without thinking of its implications and appropriate impact. In fact, however, the name of 'Father' for God is foundational for Christian praying. It is the hallmark of Jesus' own relationship with God and of his prayers. Jesus' *Abba* is even more intimate, however: it was the word in Aramaic—the colloquial language Jesus spoke—used by small children to address their father, so many suggest 'daddy' as our nearest equivalent. Paul underlines the significance of calling God 'Father' in Ephesians 3:14–15. Every time Christians are referred to as 'sons' or 'children' of God, obviously the same relationship is in focus. But the word 'our' reminds us that this is not only a vertical relationship with God but a horizontal one with the community (ultimately the world) to which we belong.

'Which art in heaven'

This is not so much a postal address as an ascription of power and holiness to God. It serves to remind us of the ultimacy and sufficiency of God. The Bible refers to God in heaven to express his otherness to all human beings and even natural forces. It emphasizes his power and authority, his knowledge and supremacy.

'Hallowed be thy name'

God's name is holy, by definition, but Jesus calls us to pause and reverence God before we think of ourselves or other people. The recognition that God is holy links us with the Old Testament and the traditions of Israel. It reminds us of Isaiah's call to service (see Isaiah 6) but also of the need to tread carefully lest we fail to honour the name or take it in vain (see Exodus 20:7). Yet it also links us into the saints of the New Testament and the early Church who were, as Paul said, 'called to be holy' (Romans 1:7). The alignment of ourselves with the holiness of God must mean, however, that we surrender our own sinful and finite perspectives as we come to prayer. Properly understood, the affirmation 'Hallowed be thy name' means that all our praying should pass through the filter of God's purity before we utter a word or even allow a longing to slide through our minds. Perhaps the best commentary on this line is Jesus' prayer in John 17, where he shows that hallowing God's name can be a very costly business: 'I am sending them into the world, just as you sent me. I have given myself completely for their sake, so that they may belong completely to the truth' (John 17:18–19, CEV).

The way Jesus 'sanctifies' himself or, as the CEV puts it, 'gives himself completely', for the disciples is by his life of obedience to God and finally by his death on the cross.

'Thy kingdom come. Thy will be done on earth, as it is in heaven'

These two lines both really express the same reality. Jesus' message was focused on the coming of the Kingdom, which is the realm where God's purposes are being carried out. By praying in this way, we are expressing our desire to put God's purposes before our own.

'Give us this day our daily bread'

This request reflects Jesus' claim that if we seek God's kingdom first, everything we need will be given to us (Matthew 6:33). It also serves to remind us of God's dealings with Israel in the wilderness, when God provided daily manna. Through this request we recognize our dependence on God for all our physical needs, and we also affirm that God is interested in this aspect of our being. He made us in his image from the dust of the earth and he cares for that 'dusty', physical side of us. Work and its proper rewards are surrendered to his concerns. Again, the word 'us' rules out the selfish way of praying only for our own individual needs.

'Forgive us our debts, as we forgive our debtors'

I always find it surprising that 'confession' waits so long before putting in an appearance in this prayer. Normally, when we pray, we would move to it from a focus on our own 'unholiness'. Why this delay? One possibility is that by placing it here Jesus underlines that it is as vital for our living as our 'daily bread'. Forgiveness is a daily need too, and one that flows from God. And the expectation of receiving forgiveness is in some way conditioned by our willingness to give it to others. Again, this concurs with much of Jesus' teaching (see Matthew 18:21–35).

'Debts' is sometimes translated as 'sins', and 'debtors' along the lines of 'those who sin against us' (for example, in the *Alternative Service Book 1980*), but the older word reminds us of the reality that in Jesus' world people could die in prison because of their debts.

'Lead us not into temptation, but deliver us from evil'

If, when we attempt to gaze into heaven and glimpse the holiness of God, we face something ultimately indescribable, here we are confronted with the opposite mystery—that of evil. Why do we need to pray that God would not lead us into temptation? Surely a good God should not even think about it? Some versions of this prayer use the more neutral words 'time of testing', which may appear to solve the problem. But I am not convinced. What about the more precise word 'tribulation', referring to the persecution that was expected in some forms of Jewish thought as a prelude to the coming of the Messiah? Again, this does not deal with the fundamental issue that the text implies: God may draw us into situations of danger or destruction of a physical or spiritual kind, so we need to appeal to him not to do this. The converse of this phrase, the positive request, is 'Deliver us from evil'. This seems less controversial. But why should we need to ask God to do this? The whole idea takes us back to the starting point in praying for God's will to be done. Prayer is inviting God to do what is best. He waits to be asked because he values our free will.

'For thine is the kingdom, and the power, and the glory, for ever, Amen'

This is a wonderful ascription to God, but does not occur in the original text. It is part of the Authorized Version's translation of Matthew's Gospel (Matthew 6:13) but is not in the earliest manuscripts. It was probably added from passages such as 1 Chronicles 29:11 and Revelation 4:11 as the prayer was used more and more in the liturgies of the churches. Although it may not have come to us from Jesus, it is appropriate that we should return our gaze completely to God with whom we began.

Each of these phrases of the Lord's Prayer can be expanded as a way of 'praying the Bible', and here are some suggestions of how to do that:

'Our Father in heaven'

Reflect on scriptures which express:
- God's care for us
- God's greatness

Perhaps these scriptures could be read alternately.

'Give us this day our daily bread'

- Thank God for his provision for our physical needs—food, water, clothes, warmth and health. You can continue to expand this by including emotional and relational needs too, although we remain focused overall on the physical.
- Pray for those involved in providing food—research and development, farmers, manufacturers, distributors, shops, those who cook.
- Pray for the countries from which your favourite foods come.
- Pray for those who have little food and for agencies such as CAFOD, Christian Aid and Tear Fund, who seek to bring daily food to others.

'Forgive us our debts, as we forgive...'

- Spend some time reflecting on your life (especially significant moments of forgiveness, pain, guilt or the struggle to forgive others).
- Thank God for Jesus' death and resurrection.
- Forgive (or ask God to help you forgive) those who have wronged you.
- Pray for situations where the need for forgiveness is urgent—domestic (parent/child, husband/wife); national (look in the daily newspapers); international (the Balkans, Israel/Palestine, Sierra Leone, Rwanda, Nigeria, Northern Ireland, Afghanistan and so on).

'Deliver us from evil'

- Pray for those you know who are struggling with temptations. (It may be best, even if you are in a group, to do this silently, for reasons of confidentiality.)
- Ask God to help you with areas where you know you are struggling and pray for people you find difficult to love.
- Pray for people trapped in difficult situations (social deprivation, drugs, crime, hopelessness).
- Pray for those who seek to help them (Prison Fellowships, Christians working in rehabilitation centres).

CONVERSION

In recent years another helpful way to pray the Bible has been provided by Michael Perry, an Anglican priest, as well as the author of several books, including *The Dramatised Bible*, which in different ways can help us engage with the Bible. Michael Perry takes scripture and adapts it for prayer, gathering passages from many parts of the Bible and grouping them under headings such as Approach, Confession, For Others, For Ourselves, and Blessing. Here is an illustration from his book, *Bible Praying* (HarperCollins, 1992, pages 78 and 277). It comes from the Confession section and is based on Hosea 14:1–2.

O Lord our God,
our sins have been our downfall,
but now we turn to you and confess them:
forgive us our sins
and receive our prayers
that we may praise you once again;
through Jesus Christ our Lord. Amen.

Here is a Blessing, taken from 1 Corinthians 16:13–14:

Be on your guard,
stand firm in the faith,
be people of courage,
be strong,
do everything in love;
and the grace of the Lord Jesus
be with you always. Amen.

These examples provide us with a model to help devise our own prayers. From the many suitable passages, here are two from the Old Testament and two from the New Testament:

Exodus 34:5–9a	Luke 24:28–34
Isaiah 43:1–7	Ephesians 6:1–14

Read your chosen passage several times, bearing in mind the context in which you want the prayer to be used: is it for personal devotion or a small group, or for responsive praying in a church service? Also think about which is the clearest translation for your purpose. Do you want poetic language or more of a prose style?

Once you have decided on the most appropriate translation for the context, then you can start work, first asking God to help you. Call to mind the context, thinking of the people who will be there if you know the situation well. Next re-read the passage either aloud or silently. If you have a good memory, it can be even more effective to recall the words; another approach is to record the passage and then play it back to yourself. (Don't be afraid to experiment.) Pause when insights or ways of adapting the prayer come to mind, but do not yet write them down.

Eventually it is time to write the scripture out in a prayer form. Often, some of it flows easily into a prayer and some doesn't. Deal with the parts that seem to 'want to be prayed', then come back and struggle with those that are more resistant. It can sometimes be hard work, so don't be put off. Remember that in the struggle you are also praying! There is no need to include everything from the passage in your prayer, although you should take care that you are not distorting the sense if you do omit parts of it.

We can also sometimes use a different mode for the prayer. For instance, the passage may be about the goodness of God and his gifts to us. So the prayer could be in the mode of praise and thanksgiving. But it could also be used to form a prayer of confession on the basis that we have forgotten that God has given 'all these things' or perhaps that we have misused them.

EXPANSION

Another way to use scripture is to let a passage from the Bible provide you with the headings for your own prayers, taking each line or even phrase and allowing it to prompt you with a mini-meditation.

Take the simple sentence, 'Jesus' disciples were arguing about which one of them was the greatest' (Luke 9:46, CEV). We could begin with praise for Jesus, his life, death and resurrection, who he is and what he means to us. We could then give thanks that he calls people like us to be his disciples. We could pray for a church we know that is divided ('which of them was the greatest') or we might want to pray for fellow disciples who are struggling to live up to their calling. We could move on to praying for people and nations where there is conflict, or, after thanking God for Jesus, we might wish to pray for the group of disciples or church to which we belong. We could ask God to deal with issues that perplex us or that are causing division. Alternatively, the small-mindedness of the disciples might prompt us to a time of personal reflection and confession, or indeed we could pray for some of the sins that beset the Church.

THEMED PRAYERS

In recent years, 'themed' cafés and pubs have become all the rage. The rooms are given a particular ambience, or, for example, Irish pubs or '60s cafés are dressed to reflect that particular culture. In a similar way we can use verses from various parts of the Bible that carry a common theme or image and use them to form our prayers.

'Light' is an obvious example. A prayer based on light could look like this:

God said, 'Let there be light' and there was light.
Father, we praise you that you are the source of all light.
God said, 'Let there be the sun by day and the moon by night.'
Father, we praise you for the gift of each new day and for the our night-time rest.

Jesus said, 'I am the Light of the world.'
Father, we thank you for the spiritual illumination that we find in Jesus.
Jesus said, 'You are the light of the world.'
Living Lord, we thank you that you send us to bring your hope, love and truth into our world.

Paul said, 'You are to shine like stars in a dark world.'

    Father, forgive us that so often we do not bring joy and integrity into the dull and compromised situations in which we work and live.

John said, 'Whoever loves his brother lives in the light, but whoever hates his brother is in the darkness.'

    Holy Spirit, create in us your fruit of love so that we may truly live in the light and honour him who is the Light of the world.
In Jesus' name, Amen.

Other themes that can be developed prayerfully are love, truth, hope, faith, courage, service and community. One way to do this is firstly to gather together a list of appropriate verses, either by brainstorming or using a concordance.

Secondly, decide what form of prayer will be most appropriate. Will it be a responsive prayer, for example, and will any of the verses be a helpful basis for the response(s)? In our prayer on the theme of light, we could use, 'God is light: and in him there is no darkness'. Either the people could say the whole sentence, or a leader could use the words up to the colon and this would prompt the rest of us to pray the second half as a response.

Also see if the verses can be grouped so as to give clear structure to the prayer.

Alternatively, if you are in a group which is used to praying together in an extempore way, you may find it more creative to agree on a theme and then ask the Holy Spirit to guide you. Wait in silence for, say, five minutes. You could invite people to speak out scriptures on the theme, which have come to mind. Then allow the prayers to flow. At the end of this period of open prayer, summarize the main issues that have emerged in a concluding prayer.

There are special values in praying like this. For instance, scripture can provide us with a more comprehensive structure and content to our prayers than we might manage alone. The process of using scripture serves to remind us that we belong to a community of faith, and this serves to support us as we pray. Personally, I find that using scripture provides God with an opportunity to challenge me, even as I pray. If you are in a group, please share your own experiences and insights concerning the use of scripture in prayer. If you are on your own and have the Book of Common Prayer or a modern equivalent, look at some of the Collects and work out how they are rooted in scripture. Is this one reason why they have resourced Christians for so long in their praying?

Sing

Those of you from liturgical traditions will realize that often there is a fine line between praying and singing. That is true for praying or singing parts of the Bible too. The Magnificat and Benedictus are prime examples. Many modern songs also use scripture and can be an effective way of praying. What are the advantages of singing scripture for prayer?

FURTHER AFIELD

Arrange to visit a monastery or other Christian community and find out about their prayer life. An ideal visit will include sharing in the corporate prayer times, hearing something about the overall pattern of prayer for that community and how they see it relating to the rest of their life, and spending some time talking with individual members to find out what a life of prayer does for them. It may be helpful to work out some questions you would like answered before you go, but always give those you talk with opportunity to share their own hearts too. Then, when you return, in some way try to share in the prayer life of the group you have visited.

PRAYER

*Father God, how we thank you that through the Bible we know you are a
God who longs not only to speak to us but to hear our answering cries*
of love,
of praise
and of need.

Son of God, how we thank you that you have taught us how to pray,
through the stories you told,
through the prayer you taught
and even through the dark night of your agonies.

Spirit of God, how we thank you that you are beside us and within us
to prompt us to pray when we are prayerless,
to direct us in prayer when we are confused
and to release us for prayer when we are lost for words.

*Father, Son and Holy Spirit, how we thank you for the resources of the
scriptures for our prayers:*
for its words and images to use,
for its prayers to refresh
and for its promises to sustain.

Amen.

Chapter 7

STUDY IT

ICE-BREAKERS

1. What was your favourite subject at school and why?
2. Has the Bible ever helped you to sort out a problem in your life? If so, and you are in a group, share this with other people if you feel able.
3. Have you ever read through the Bible in a year? What were the problems and what were the benefits?
4. What have you found to be the best help to studying the Bible? Either invite people to explain or ask them beforehand to bring along their example to the session to explain to the group.

INTRODUCTION

'Learning to play, playing to learn'—these words slowly passed by me as I was driving along a motorway, on the side of a green lorry that was supplying toys to a well-known chain store for younger children. But they are words we do well to note. All around us there are learning opportunities—'history zones' on television, and all these enticing websites encouraging us to learn everything about everything. Sometimes learning from or about the Bible can seem boring rather than enjoyable

—but it needn't be like that, even for those who are 'new media'-illiterate. In this chapter we are going to consider some simple, 'low-tech' approaches to Bible study which should prove enjoyable and stimulating. But first a 'Bible study' about studying the Bible.

BIBLE STUDY

2 TIMOTHY 3:14–17

There are many passages we could turn to, but in 2 Timothy we eavesdrop on a conversation between one of the most adventurous men ever, and a more timid one. Paul, the adventurous one, has survived storms that make white-water rafting look tame. He has explored many parts of the known world and would have made fascinating TV or radio travel programmes because of all the trouble he got into (see 2 Corinthians 11:23–27). But the study programme he commends to Timothy, his younger, more nervous friend, is his Bible. Why?

- There is enough to study for a lifetime. Ever since Timothy was a child he has been exploring and discovering the great riches in the Bible (v. 15: of course, the 'Holy Scriptures' were what we describe as the Old Testament), but there is enough there to keep him going for the rest of his life.
- There is a wealth of insight and understanding to gain. People who have studied the scriptures before him can pass on many fruitful insights ('You know who your teachers were', v. 14), and there is always something to pass on to others ('teach the message of God's truth', 2 Timothy 2:15). Indeed, scripture needs a continuous succession of teachers because it is so vital and stimulating: 'Take the teachings that you heard me proclaim... and entrust them to reliable people, who will be able to teach others also' (2:2).
- The scriptures relate to the most important issue in the world and for the world, for the 'Holy Scriptures... are able to give the wisdom that leads to salvation' (v. 15).

- The source of these scriptures is none other than God himself (v. 16).
- They provide degree and vocational qualifications and equipment rolled into one (v. 17) for living a full and proper human life (v. 16).

It is worth taking a closer look at verse 16. Paul explains four ways in which the Bible is useful to the teacher, and this implies that it will also achieve these four things for others who learn from it:

- **Teaching the truth:** that is, positive understanding of the nature of God and people—what we would call Christian doctrine. Understanding the true nature of God is also the key to understanding people.
- **Rebuking error:** that is, correcting false concepts and understandings of God and people.
- **Correcting faults:** that is, showing what are false, inadequate and wrong attitudes and ways of behaving.
- **Instruction for right living:** that is, the proper way to think about and treat other people.

So now for some 'study'! Encourage everyone in the group to think of four passages from the Old Testament—one to illustrate each of the four ways in which the Bible is useful. When you have done this, share your reflections.

There has probably never been a time when people have been more challenged to go on learning—this is true in the workplace as well as for leisure time. It is also vital that Christians respond to this challenge and the opportunities that come with it. Part of our task is simply to know the Bible, because it is the foundational document for our faith and community. We need it if we are to relate honestly, sympathetically and constructively to other people, especially those of other faiths or those who are involved in a spiritual search. However, we also need to study it, to deepen our own understanding and our ability to relate the Bible to our changing world. To cover all this is impossible in a chapter, so we will concentrate on a few ways to look afresh at the Bible itself.

COMPARING PARALLEL PASSAGES

One way to discover new insights about the Bible is to examine carefully passages where we have two or more differing accounts of apparently the same event, story, sayings or even sets of laws. I find that such an approach is great fun and can be very illuminating. It requires careful attention and, as in any detective work, small clues can be highly important.

In case you are wondering whether the differences really matter, consider the Gospels, where there are many such parallel passages. We have three Gospels that follow a similar pattern—Matthew, Mark, Luke (because of their common perspective, they are often called the 'Synoptics', meaning 'seen with the same eye')—and John, which is very individual. Comparisons between the Gospels have kept scholars busy for more than a hundred years. One of the most important comparisons to look at is between the different accounts of the resurrection of Jesus, which were famously investigated by a journalist, Frank Morison, who wanted to prove that the resurrection did not happen. He came away from his research a convinced Christian, because the more he studied the variations between the Gospels, the more the whole event looked authentic—and he wrote a book on the subject, called *Who Moved the Stone?* (Faber and Faber, 1930).

Studying all the resurrection accounts is clearly both hugely significant for the Christian faith and immensely complex, but it is important to realize that the same approach can apply to other parts of the Bible too. One example is the so-called 'Ten Commandments', which are found in the Old Testament and which have been vitally important for Jewish, Christian and other faiths (Islam and, less directly, Sikhism and Hinduism.

THE TEN COMMANDMENTS

In addition to the specific commandments given in various places within the Bible, we have two versions of the 'Ten Commandments' which, interestingly, are not exactly the same. You can find them in Exodus 20:1–17 and Deuteronomy 5:6–21.

Have a careful read and see if you can spot at least three differences. Why do you think there are differences?

- Is it because you are using different translations, or that different words were needed to convey the same meaning at different times in Israel's history?
- Is it because the two versions were given at different times? (In Exodus, Moses is reporting what God had said to him on Sinai, immediately before the people enter into their covenant with him, whereas in Deuteronomy Moses is speaking to the Israelites before they enter the Promised Land.)
- Is it because one represents the spoken version and the other the version carved in stone (Exodus 24:12), or because there were two versions anyway (Deuteronomy 34:1–4)?
- Is it because they were used on different occasions or by different groups of people (one in the south and one in the north, for instance)?
- Is it that one is right and the other wrong? If so, why did the Hebrew scribes, who were so careful, not make them exactly the same?

What are the 'Ten' Commandments? If you look carefully at the Deuteronomy 5 version, there could be twelve: can you find them all? Or maybe there are even more? (If you want a clue, think especially about verses 8–10, 15 and 21.) Come to think of it, where does it say there are 'ten'? (Try Exodus 34:28; Deuteronomy 4:13; 10:4.)

Let's now look at one big difference between the two accounts. Look closely at Exodus 20:8–11 and Deuteronomy 5:12–15. The big difference here is the explanation given as to why the Sabbath is to be a special day. (There are some small differences here as well so if you are a 'details' person and like detective work, please track them down!) In Exodus, the reason is to do with the way God created the world: 'On the seventh day I rested. That is why I, the Lord, blessed the Sabbath' (v. 11), whereas in Deuteronomy it is because God rescued them from slavery (v. 15). So in the first case it is a commandment linked to creation and in the second it is linked to salvation. In the first case, we are told to model God's behaviour in refraining from activity; in the second there appears almost to be a 'humanitarian' motive ('God gave you rest from slavery so you must give your slaves a rest'). That is not quite how it is presented, however; rather it is to do with remembering God's acts of redemption.

Why does the difference matter? One way in which it has mattered is that in some church traditions this commandment has been regarded as a 'moral' commandment (because of the 'humanitarian' reference), and therefore valid for all times; and in other traditions as a 'ritual' commandment from which we have been released because we are in the new covenant. The scope of the commandment might be significant in another way. If it is justified on the basis of the created order, then it has universal application, but if it is justified in terms of God's covenant with Israel (because he rescued them from Egypt), then it would be applicable only to those who belong to the covenant.

THE GOSPELS

Small differences

We can see small differences between parallel Gospel passages, in terms of both context and content. For an example of a difference in *context*, we look at Matthew 18:12–14 and Luke 15:1–7.

Matthew and Luke record what is basically the same story from Jesus, the one we normally call the parable of the lost sheep. In Matthew's Gospel it is related to not 'despising' 'little ones' (18:10), whereas in Luke it is about God's care for sinners (15:2). Is this because Jesus used the story more than once in different contexts? Is it because the people who retold Jesus' stories before the Gospels were written down applied it to different situations? Or is it because the two stories are referring to the same people but using different language? 'Despising little ones' could mean rejecting or looking down on people who were marginalized, such as the 'outcasts' whom Jesus welcomed. Or do you think there is another way to explain the differences between the two Gospels?

For a small difference in *content*, we can look at Matthew 5:3 and Luke 6:20. The significant difference between these passages is that Matthew mentions that the 'spiritually poor' are blessed, while Luke simply has 'poor'. Luke always seems to take a special interest in those who are poor (for instance, Luke's Christmas story has shepherds, whereas Matthew has the Magi with their splendid gifts). It is possible, once again, that both Gospels are denoting the same group of people, but this is not necessarily so. Matthew's version might lead us to an acknowledgment of spiritual poverty as a pre-condition for entering the Kingdom—and so could lead on to the idea of justification by faith alone with repentance as a pre-condition; whereas Luke could lead us either to renounce all wealth—as do some monastic orders—or to focus all our energy on helping the under-privileged.

To say that these are 'small differences' is *not* to say that they are inconsequential. Obviously, the way we understand all these passages, and the interpretation to which we choose to give priority, can make a huge difference to the focus of our Christian lives.

Big differences

We will now look at two examples where there are big differences between the four Gospel accounts—Jesus' entry into Jerusalem, and his 'words from the cross'.

There are four accounts of Jesus entering Jerusalem prior to the week of his death and resurrection: Matthew 21:1–11; Mark 11:1–11; Luke 19:28–40; and John 12:12–19.

We will look particularly at Luke's and John's accounts, dealing with some of the major differences:

• John's Gospel does not include the account of the two disciples being sent to the village to bring back the animal (in Luke 'a colt'), only that Jesus 'found a donkey'. Does this alter the story at all, only a little or a lot? What difference does it make? It is also worthy of note that in John Jesus rides on the donkey in response to the crowd's acclaim (vv. 13–14), whereas in Luke Jesus' action precedes this praise.

- Luke's Gospel tells the story from the viewpoint of people travelling with Jesus into Jerusalem (v. 36). John's Gospel recounts it with an emphasis on people coming out of Jerusalem (vv. 12–13). Could both have been true historically or are they contradictory? If both are possible, why do these Gospels give different perspectives? At its simplest, for Luke Jesus is claiming to be king, while in John he is being acknowledged as king and welcomed to his own city. Does this alter the way we view the crucifixion?
- John (v. 15) refers to the quotation from Zechariah about the king riding on a donkey, whereas Luke does not. Is this because Luke did not want to present Jesus as someone who provoked the Roman authorities by making such a claim? (See Luke 1:1–4: 'Theophilus' may have been a high-ranking Roman.) John says that the disciples understood this reference to the scriptures only after the resurrection and that they had 'done this for him' (v. 16).

On Good Friday, many churches hold services which relate to the sayings and prayers of Jesus from the cross. Traditionally these are known as the seven words from the cross. No Gospel has all seven, however; they are spread out between the four Gospels. Look at the different accounts (Matthew 27:32–50; Mark 15 :21–38; Luke 23:32–46; John 19:17–37) and note in which Gospel each of the 'words' occur. Then construct a chart showing where each saying occurs by listing the sayings on the left-hand side of a sheet of paper and the names of the four Gospels across the top, and placing a tick every time the saying occurs. Think especially about those that occur in only one Gospel, and ask yourself, does this saying fit other special features or interests of that Gospel?

OTHER WAYS TO ACCESS THE BIBLE

Here I can only give a few guidelines, but there are many other tools and resources to help you and a number of these will be found in the Resources section.

WORD STUDIES

Trace the different ways particular words are used in the Bible. Words like 'grace', 'glory', 'image', 'justice' and 'love' are obvious choices. A concordance or computer word search facility is a great help here.

As an illustration, let us think about the word 'image' as used in the Authorized Version. Immediately we become aware that this is used in both a good and a bad sense. So we can study the positive uses relating to the 'image of God', by looking at passages like Genesis 1:26–27 (bearing in mind 5:1 and 3); 1 Corinthians 11:7; Romans 8:29; 2 Corinthians 3:18; 4:4; Colossians 1:15; 3:10). We can think about issues such as whether this 'image of God' is a mark of all human beings, in what ways it is uniquely applied to Jesus, and how the Bible suggests we can recapture this image for ourselves.

We can then conduct a parallel study looking at passages where the word 'image' refers to idols. We might think about the dangers of such images, and whether making images is itself prohibited or whether the prohibition is only about worshipping them. We can also see whether the Bible takes the same view about images (in the sense of idols) all the way through.

CHARACTER STUDIES

Character studies are similar to word studies. People tend to be fascinated by people, so this is an appealing and intriguing approach. We need to be careful, though, not to end up more fascinated with the people than with the God whose story they accompany! We also need to be aware that just because the Bible relates a story, it is not necessarily commending the characters involved.

THEME STUDIES

With this we follow issues or concepts and not just words. So, if we were studying the Holy Spirit we would also look for passages about the 'Paraclete' or 'Comforter'. If our theme was 'how God guides us', as well as looking at passages dealing with 'guidance', instruction' or 'God's will', we could look at stories where God's guidance is seen to be at work, such as Genesis 22:1–19; Acts 10; 16:6–34; 21:7–16. Other themes or subjects we might wish to look at are 'attitudes to death', 'marriage and divorce', 'older people', 'gifts, human and divine' —but the list is endless.

Another thematic approach is to look at a biblical image or symbol to try to understand it more fully. I've given below an example based around 'fire'.

Read Exodus 3:1–11 or Isaiah 6:1–10 or Acts 2:1–18. Fire is a very important symbol in the Bible. In speaking of it as a symbol, I do not mean that 'fire' in the Bible has nothing to do with ignition and flames and burning, but rather that it often carries a powerful message as well. There are two main messages that come with fire. One is the obvious one about destruction and judgment, either by human authorities or by God. The other is to do with release to and acceptance by God. Along with this second meaning, fire comes to have a strong association with God's presence itself.

Here are four passages to illustrate each of these meanings.

A. Destruction and judgment by humans

Nebuchadnezzar carried off everything that was left in the temple; he robbed the treasury and the personal storerooms of the king and his officials. He took everything back to Babylon. Nebuchadnezzar's troops burnt down the temple and destroyed every important building in the city. Then they broke down the city wall. The survivors were taken to Babylon as prisoners.
2 CHRONICLES 36:18–20, CEV

B. Destruction and judgment by God

The two angels said to Lot, 'The Lord has heard many terrible things about the people of Sodom, and he has sent us here to destroy the city.' ... The sun was coming up as Lot reached the town of Zoar, and the Lord sent burning

sulphur down like rain on Sodom and Gomorrah. He destroyed those cities and everyone who lived in them, as well as their land and the trees and grass that grew there.
GENESIS 19:12–13, 23–25, CEV

C. Release and acceptance by God

When it was time for the evening sacrifice, Elijah prayed: 'Our Lord, you are the God of Abraham, Isaac, and Israel. Now, prove that you are the God of this nation, and that I, your servant, have done this at your command. Please answer me, so these people will know that you are the Lord God, and that you will turn back their hearts to you.' The Lord immediately sent fire, and it burnt up the sacrifice, the wood, and the stones. It scorched the ground everywhere around the altar and dried up every drop of water in the ditch. When the crowd saw what had happened, they all bowed down and shouted, 'The Lord is God! The Lord is God!'
1 KINGS 18:36–39, CEV

D. God's holy presence

On the morning of the third day there was thunder and lightning. A thick cloud covered the mountain, a loud trumpet blast was heard, and everyone in camp trembled with fear. Moses led them out of the camp to meet God, and they stood at the foot of the mountain. Mount Sinai was covered with smoke because the Lord had come down in a flaming fire. Smoke poured out of the mountain just like a furnace, and the whole mountain shook.
EXODUS 19:16–18

Now read each of the following twelve passages and decide whether it is an A, B, C or D-type passage. You should end up with three of each.

Exodus 13:21	2 Kings 1:10	Isaiah 6:2
Leviticus 9:24	1 Chronicles 21:26	Luke 12:49
Leviticus 10:2	2 Chronicles 7:1	2 Thessalonians 1:8
Deuteronomy 4:36	Psalms 74:4–8	James 3:6

If you fancy playing with fire a little more, here is a further investigation.

• It isn't always easy to be sure into which of the four categories above (or, indeed, additional ones we might discover) any particular reference to fire fits. Can you work out a pattern or set of connections that illustrates how one category slides over into the other(s)? For instance, a possibility is that because fire is associated with God— as a sign of his presence—it could be used as a sign of destruction against his enemies and security/blessing for those in his favour, because by threatening or destroying enemies he blesses his favoured ones. On the other hand, the blessing might simply come because to be near a fire in the dark and cold is comforting and warming. Which is it, or could it be both?

• Often, those who are enemies of God have thought that by destroying God's people (by fire and other means) they would put an end to them. But God seems to use that destruction to release the impact of his people on a wider scale. Remember the famous phrase, 'The blood of the martyrs is the seed of the church' (Tertullian).

• In what other ways does fire function? What other metaphors are associated with it, and what other messages does it carry? Why is fire sometimes positive and sometimes negative in its implications and associations?

BACK TO BASICS

Whatever approach we are using in our study of any Bible passages, before assuming that the way we are used to understanding them is right, it is useful to try to discover what the passages meant to the people who first wrote or heard them. Often, our way of seeing things is influenced by our church traditions, which can be insightful, but our understanding may also be distorted as a result of living in a different culture from the one in which the Bible originated. We may then misread what is important. As well as finding out what a passage meant initially, it is also important to notice changes in understanding at different times and in different parts of the Bible, especially working out how the New Testament's views differ from the Old. The following exercise is one way to start this awareness.

THE ALTERNATIVE VERSION

The purpose of this exercise is to discover how passages are re-used within the Bible. Look up passages dealing with the Exodus story (a concordance will give you help, as will a topical concordance) and see how different elements and emphases are used in different places. Or read Jesus' Sermon on the Mount (Matthew 5—7) and note how he re-uses Old Testament passages: the phrase 'but I say to you...' is the signal for spotting this!

DAY BY DAY

There are several organizations, such as BRF, IBRA, Scripture Union, Crusade for World Revival (*Every Day with Jesus*) and Bible Alive, which provide guidance notes on reading the Bible every (or almost every) day. Using these publications over a number of years is an excellent way to study the Bible. The notes will ensure that a wide range of material is covered, and because they are prepared for people with different levels of knowledge about the Bible, it is fairly easy, by changing from one type of notes to another, to keep extending your understanding. They will provide historical background as well as points to apply to our lives today. Most also help us to respond to God. It is always beneficial if a small group can meet to share what they are learning from their Bible reading notes: this means that we can help each other not only to understand but also to live out what we are learning.

Finally, it is worth checking what we have learnt against the four points Paul makes to Timothy (see page 110). In more modern speech, we could say:

• What have I/we learnt about God, people, behaviour and anything else?

- What adjustments do I/we need to make to the way I/we have been thinking?
- What behaviour do I/we now need to put right in the light of what I/we have discovered?
- What should I/we do (or consider doing) that I/we have not been doing?

FURTHER AFIELD

- Visit your local Christian bookshop and talk to the people there about the wide range of books and study aids to help people understand the Bible better. If you are not already familiar with Bible resources for computers, they may well be able to advise you or even arrange a demonstration. If not, then the next few paragraphs may help you.

The first development for computers was the text of the Bible available electronically on CD-ROM. Now, one CD-ROM not only has four English versions, and the original Greek and Hebrew but eleven Asian languages too. It has a search facility, and parallel texts can be displayed in synchronized windows. Imagine how helpful this can be for Asian pastors whose Bible study aids may be in English but whose primary language is an indigenous one, or evangelists who operate in cross-cultural situations. For instance, a Korean missionary in Bangladesh will be able to prepare studies in the local language with parallel passages in Korean. Instead of a small library of books all he or she has to carry is one CD-ROM—and a computer!

In the UK, *Quick Verse* (version 6) has eleven Bibles. When I looked, it was retailing at £129, which is not quite as accessible as the Asian version mentioned above, which sells for only $10 and has the Greek and Hebrew as well.

If you do not wish to carry a PC around with you, then it is possible to buy software packages to go with some palm-top computers. For basic information on products, see the Christian Software Catalogue, available from most Christian bookshops.

There are also CD-ROM Bible study aids available, which can

provide commentary on the text, or search facilities so that people can relate different parts of the Bible dealing with the same character, words or themes (useful for the approaches mentioned earlier in this chapter). These aids can also include pictures of artefacts that are mentioned in the text or that provide a historical context in which to understand the passages, or maps to help contextualize the Bible.

- Consider asking a local minister or Religious Studies teacher to run a course for you on, for instance, the prophets or the Gospels. You may need to recruit others to join you to ensure the group is viable for this approach.
- Visit a suitable Bible training college—either one that is near to you or one that serves your denomination—to find out how these could be a resource for local Christians who want to study the Bible.

PRAYER

Blessed Lord, who hast caused all holy Scriptures to be written for our learning; Grant that we may in such wise hear them, read, mark, learn and inwardly digest them, that by patience, and by comfort of thy holy Word, we may embrace, and ever hold fast the blessed hope of everlasting life, which thou hast given us in our Saviour Jesus Christ. Amen
COLLECT FOR THE SECOND SUNDAY IN ADVENT, *THE BOOK OF COMMON PRAYER*

Chapter 8

DO IT

ICE-BREAKERS

1. Share your experiences of DIY. Has anything ever gone disastrously wrong? To whom do you look for help? Do you like best planning, purchasing, doing the work or showing your friends the result? Or do you just buy the magazines and dream on?
2. Have you ever done anything really difficult? Told the truth when it was unpopular, climbed Snowdon, Ben Nevis and Scafell in a day (or even one of them!), run a marathon...? Share together your recollections, including why you did it and whether you think it was worth the effort.
3. Do you find speaking a foreign language easy or hard? How do you learn them best—from books, tapes, videos or by going to the country? Have you ever found it useful to be able to speak another language? Share some experiences.

INTRODUCTION

We have seen that many parts of the Bible are presented to us as stories and that all 66 books of the Bible are in a story framework, namely God's adventure with all human beings and the world they live in. However, the biblical story is not offered to us as something that we should only appreciate and enjoy (along the lines of a novel for holiday reading, for instance), nor that we should only know it well in order to pass some kind of exam (like the Highway Code). Rather it is a story that entices and invites us to become participants in the story. Only in this way can we fully understand it. This means that we have to play our part, take part in it and live it out. Hence, it is not surprising that some parts of the Bible are guidance to be respected and commands to be obeyed. This chapter encourages us to respond to some of this type of material. It is offered as a stimulus to put parts of the Bible into practice—to 'do the Bible'.

There are three points to consider as we explore these aspects of the Bible.

- It is not always easy to know whether we are meant to obey any specific command. The Bible itself creates a significant gap between the Old and the New Testaments on the grounds that Jesus has radically transformed the basis of our relationship with God by establishing the new covenant: hence all the Old Testament regulations need to be reconsidered. Even in the New Testament itself, commands are directed to specific people in particular contexts and do not necessarily have universal applicability.
- We cannot draw a clear line between the stories and the laws. We need to remember that the laws are presented within a story and there is a growing scholarly opinion that the stories are themselves meant to form and influence our behaviour and attitudes.
- We have the Christian community and the personal insight of the Holy Spirit to help us work out how the instructions of the Bible apply to us today, as well as how they can help us to handle situations such as globalization, ecological challenges and medical dilemmas which are not directly covered by the Bible.

BIBLE STUDY

Read Philippians 4:4–9 and discuss together what this passage has to say about the following issues:

- Our inner attitudes
- Our relationships with others
- Prayer
- Our relationship with God and the consequences of it
- What we should focus our minds on

There's a lot here in a very few verses, but the most challenging instruction comes at the end (v. 9). What does Paul have to say here about our response to biblical teaching? It seems to me that it is something like this. We learn biblical teaching by hearing and seeing it lived out, but we, like Paul, also have to do it! Then we can anticipate God's blessing.

Here are some more challenging passages about doing God's word.

- Deuteronomy 30:1–20
- Isaiah 5:1–7
- Matthew 7:24–27
- James 1:19–27

Look up these passages and work out the benefits of doing God's word and the consequences of ignoring it.

From these and other passages, it is clear that the Bible was never meant, primarily, to be dissected or admired. Rather, it was meant to help people live fuller lives, which, of course, means lives that are pleasing to God. Saying this, however, is dangerous. We can hardly forget the reprimands that Jesus gave to the Pharisees because they took the laws and determined that they would work out every detail of how they must be obeyed. The Bible must not be reduced to a trade union manual or a flat-pack assembly guide. It not only cries out to be put into practice, it also provides vision and motivation.

There is another issue about 'doing' the Bible that we need to consider. We live in a Do-it-*Yourself* society. This is not only in terms of car maintenance or decorating the house. It represents a view that because everyone is equal, everyone should be able to do anything they want to. The Bible, however, constantly reminds us that we cannot do very much by ourselves. For instance, Abraham got into a real mess when he tried to pass off his wife Sarah to the Egyptian Pharaoh as his sister: he was trying to sort out a dangerous situation for himself (Genesis 12:11–20). The Bible sums up the basic attitude we need when it says, 'Trust in the Lord with all your heart, and do not rely on your own insight. In all your ways acknowledge him, and he will make straight your paths. Be not wise in your own eyes' (Proverbs 3:5–7, RSV).

In the New Testament, Peter is shown as failing when he attempts to disregard Jesus' warning that he would deny him once Jesus was arrested. Positively, the Bible emphasizes that we need the help of the Holy Spirit if we are going to become like Jesus and live God's way (see Luke 22:31–34; 54–62 and, for instance, Galatians 5:22–25).

In addition to God's help, which we need from start to finish, we need other people to *sustain* us too: we are unlikely to get far on God's journey on our own. Yet having said all of this, let me reaffirm that the Bible is meant to be a way of living, not a theoretical guide to philosophy.

In the next sections, we are going to think through what it means to 'do' the Bible. First we will underline the importance to Jesus of getting people to take God's commands seriously enough to live them out. Then we will see how the Bible has shaped some significant people's lives, before moving on to look at some of the challenges the Bible presents to those who want to 'do it'.

NEIGHBOURS

To illustrate what I mean, let's take a look at the parable of the good Samaritan, which you can find in Luke 10:25–37. The direct prompt for this brilliant story is an apparently theoretical question, 'Who is my neighbour?'

How would you define 'neighbour'? First think about this (either in your group or on your own). Does your definition include:

- The people living on either side of your house?
- The person who sits at the next desk to you at work?
- The person on the other end of a telephone?

- Patients, pupils or clients (depending on your job)?
- People in front of and behind you in the supermarket; and the person on the checkout?
- A police officer who has hauled you up for speeding and is acting in a way you consider aggressive and humiliating?
- Those living in your home?

If we live in a global village, is everyone my neighbour?

The story, as Jesus tells it, shows how people who were respected, like the priest and the Levite, failed to help the traveller who had been attacked and wounded by robbers. On the other hand, the Samaritan, who belonged to a group of people Jesus' hearers despised, proved to be compassionate and helpful in practical ways.

The implications of Jesus' story are essentially twofold. First, loving our neighbour is not a theoretical issue for debate. It is a practical, hands-on issue, both in terms of who counts as 'neighbour' and what loving them means—giving practical help, doing what needs to be done, in so far as it is in our capacity to do it. Second, it means doing what is necessary for any person who is in need, irrespective of any previous or preconceived relationship with them.

It is interesting to go back to Leviticus 19:18, where this command first occurs: 'Do not take revenge on anyone or continue to hate him, but love your neighbour as you love yourself. I am the Lord.'

Two things leap out from this verse:

- By implication, the neighbour is anyone with whom I have any kind of relationship.
- The command applies particularly if there has been some breach or damage to that relationship.

God commands me to love the very person whom I have been wanting to harm, the one who I think has caused me serious damage. It is a human tendency to restrict the term 'neighbour' to those near us, or those similar to us, or those who like us. Hence Jesus needed to challenge the narrow application of 'neighbour' through his story.

The Samaritans' relationship with the Jews was characterized by mistrust and resentment. In contrast, by his attention to the wounded Jew, the Samaritan traveller in this story shows compassion where he sees the need.

Of course, we not only have this story, we have the example of Jesus, who frequently acted like the Samaritan.

- **Matthew 8:5–13:** Jesus heals a Roman soldier's servant. Not only does Jesus help people in need, but he is willing to help a Roman soldier and his servant, even though the Romans were the occupying force in his country.
- **Luke 9:51–55:** When Jesus and his disciples are refused hospitality by some Samaritans, and the disciples want to call down divine judgment on them, it is the disciples who are reprimanded. It was a social obligation to provide hospitality to travellers, but Jesus' words imply that we must love even those who refuse their obligations towards us.
- **Luke 22:49–51:** Jesus heals the dismembered ear of one of those who have come to arrest him. Here again, Jesus helps the one who is acting as 'the enemy'.
- **Luke 23:34:** Jesus asks God to forgive those who have been responsible for crucifying him. In this way he seeks to protect from retribution those who are killing him.

When people manage to take Jesus' command seriously, it has very important consequences. It frequently leads to a change in relationship not only between the individuals but also between the groups they represent and whose hostilities have caused the problem. So, for instance, when Gordon Wilson publicly forgave those who killed his daughter at Enniskillen, Northern Ireland, in 1987, for some people it contributed to the dissolution of the hatred between Republicans and Unionists. The educational video *Test of Time* (BBC Education/Bible Society) contains other illustrations of the power of this kind of forgiveness. The video and the accompanying workbook for teachers are both available from Bible Society.

We can also see situations on an international scale which cry out for this kind of loving if there is to be any chance of reconciliation and rebuilding. As well as Northern Ireland, the Balkan countries, Afghanistan and Rwanda are just three parts of the world that spring to mind in this context. It is easy for us to say, 'Why can't they see that learning to love each other is the only way?' On the other hand, if we are personally challenged in this way it is tempting to say, 'I can't do that. They would take advantage of me. I would look a fool!'

What the parable of the good Samaritan seems to underline is the fact that Jesus actually meant we should 'do' the Bible. Such an approach corresponds to Jesus' instructions about his 'Bible' (which was what we call the Old Testament—see Matthew 5:17–20) and also to his own teachings: 'But anyone who hears these words of mine and does not obey them is like a foolish man who built his house on sand' (Matthew 7:26).

The same emphasis on doing is clear in the letters to the first Christian communities. So, for instance, James says, 'Do not deceive yourselves by just listening to his word; instead put it into practice' (James 1:22).

According to the Bible, it is not enough to read the Bible (or even write books about it!). We need to put it into practice. This chapter is about finding ways of 'doing' bits of the Bible, and it is worth discovering how powerful the Bible can be when people respond to it in this way, by looking briefly at some who have significantly shaped our society.

LIVING BY THE WORD

W.H. Boreham trained for the Baptist ministry at Spurgeon's College and then moved to his lifetime's work in New Zealand. He realized that religion and reality belonged together and that the Bible was the key to both.

In one of his many books illustrating this theme,[11] he wrote 23 chapters on people who were inspired by particular scriptural texts. Some of these people are well known, some not so well known. Eight of them are listed here with a very brief biographical comment on each one, followed by a list of the eight verses of scripture that Boreham saw as being their inspiration and guide. But the verses are not in the same order as the people to whom they correspond.

Which passage do you think fits best with which person?

People

A Sir Walter Scott, prolific author of the early 19th century.
B Martin Luther, famous leader of the Reformation in Germany.
C Sir John Franklin, an early 19th-century explorer.
D John Bunyan, 17th-century Christian writer, most famous for his allegorical journey tale, *The Pilgrim's Progress*.
E John Wesley, the itinerant preacher who was the catalyst for the rise of the Methodist Church.
F William Cowper, poet and hymn writer from the 18th century.
G William Carey, 18th-century linguist and pioneer missionary in India.
H William Wilberforce, early 19th-century politician who, with his colleagues from The Clapham Sect, introduced many beneficial social reforms, most notably anti-slavery legislation.

Texts

I have quoted the texts in the Authorized Version, partly because it is the form used by Boreham and partly because it was the translation with which most of these people would have been familiar.

Isaiah 43:2: When thou passest through the waters, I will be with thee; and through the rivers, they shall not overflow thee: when thou walkest through the fire, thou shalt not be burned.

Isaiah 54:2: Enlarge the place of thy tent, and let them stretch forth the curtains of thine habitations: spare not, lengthen thy cords, and strengthen thy stakes.

Mark 12:34:	And when Jesus saw that he [the scribe who asked about the greatest commandments] answered discreetly, he said unto him, Thou art not far from the kingdom of God.
Luke 18:13:	God be merciful to me a sinner.
John 6:37:	All that the Father giveth me shall come to me; and him that cometh to me I will in no wise cast out.
John 9:4:	I must work the works of him that sent me, while it is day; the night cometh, when no man can work.
Romans 1:17:	For therein is the righteousness of God revealed from faith to faith: as it is written, The just shall live by faith.
Romans 3:24:	Being justified freely by his grace through the redemption that is in Christ Jesus.

You can find the answers at the back of the book (p. 160).

So how did you get on? Were you surprised to discover which text was the guiding light for each of these people, or were they predictable? Were you surprised that such people were strongly influenced by the Bible? Why do you think they were so powerfully impacted by it?

Do you think they responded to the text only as if it were a well-known saying or proverb, or do you think the text acted as a focus for what they came to believe about God?

Can you identify with one of these eight texts in particular? Is that because you admire the person who valued it, because you already live by it, or perhaps because it focuses some of your hopes and aspirations as a Christian?

If you wish to find out more about these people, here are three suggestions.

• **The marathon challenge:** Read a biography of one of the people and see whether you can discern how their text mattered to them. Look out for any ways in which the Bible played a part in their lives, such as through attending church and hearing sermons, through their education, the literature they read, or the people they admired.

- **The relay race:** If you are a member of a group, why not choose one of the people each and then feed back your discoveries to the group?
- **The pentathlon:** Read some of the original writings of one of these people and see to what extent the importance of the Bible is reflected there.

DOING IT MY WAY

We have seen that it is important to live out the scriptures, and that many people who have contributed to our culture in a whole variety of spheres have sought to do that. The real challenge of this section, however, is not to admire others but to live out the scriptures ourselves. So how can we do this authentically?

Let's start with some of the things we may already do—at least to some extent. Below is a list of directives from the first five books of the Old Testament and from the Gospels. For each one, write down or discuss a few of the ways you think you have 'done' that particular command.

- **Exodus 20:12:** Respect your father and mother.
- **Leviticus 19:36:** Use honest scales, honest weights, and honest measures.
- **Deuteronomy 6:4:** Remember this! The Lord—and the Lord alone —is our God.
- **Matthew 5:16:** Your light must shine before people, so that they will see the good things you do and praise your Father in heaven.
- **Mark 8:34:** If anyone wants to come with me [said Jesus], he must forget self, carry his cross, and follow me.
- **Luke 6:37:** Do not judge others.

HOW NOT TO 'DO' THE BIBLE

Earlier in this chapter we noted that the vast majority of scripture, even in the 'Books of the Law'—Genesis to Deuteronomy—and the four

Gospels, does not tell us directly what to do or not to do. It is more like a story that suggests or prompts or stirs the imagination to wonder (in both senses of that word). Even when there are fairly direct instructions, many Christians would not consider that they all applied to us, or that they were all intended for us to do now. This is especially true with the Old Testament, but to some extent with the New as well. Consider the verses listed below and work out, if you do not think they apply to you, why that is.

(a) **Genesis 12:1:** Leave your country, your relatives, and your father's home.
(b) **Exodus 23:14:** Celebrate three festivals a year to honour me.
(c) **Leviticus 25:36:** Do not charge them [that is, your fellow countrymen] any interest.
(d) **Numbers 15:38:** Make tassels on the corners of your garments.
(e) **Deuteronomy 22:5:** Women are not to wear men's clothing.
(f) **Matthew 5:30:** If your right hand causes you to sin, cut it off and throw it away!
(g) **Mark 10:21:** Go and sell all you have and give the money to the poor.
(h) **Luke 9:3:** Take nothing with you for the journey.
(i) **John 20:27:** Stretch out your hand and put it in my side.

Our initial responses are probably affected by two things—our common sense, and the Christian communities to which we belong and the ways they have applied the various commands and prohibitions. These are good guides but they are not foolproof. Particularly in times of cultural change and renewal of the faith, when people have approached the Bible and been prepared to look again at its insights, profound breakthroughs have occurred. So the Old Testament commands about Jubilee (a time when all debts were cancelled, Leviticus 25:8–12), together with the prohibition on charging interest, have recently had a very significant effect on the British government and much further afield with respect to Third World debt. In earlier periods, the refusal of some groups of Christians to take oaths had equally significant impacts on society. So we need to think a little further about why and when passages need to be implemented.

One reason we might think we do not need to obey particular laws is because they were addressed to the Old Testament people of God, Israel, and not to us as Christians—(b) and (c) above are illustrations of this. However, this raises the question: why, then, do we think that the Ten Commandments apply to us? In fact, there are issues to consider even within the Ten Commandments: most (though not all) Christians do not keep the Sabbath (Saturday) holy but set aside the first day of the week for worship. In parts of the New Testament (Colossians and Hebrews, for instance), it is stated that Old Testament ceremonial laws are done away with, and the Council of Jerusalem (as reported in Acts 16) moved in the same direction. Conversely, there are New Testament passages which imply that we should keep, or even intensify the scope of, the moral and social laws of the Old Testament (Matthew 5:21–48).

A second category of commands that we consider inapplicable to ourselves are those that are directed to an individual, or even a group, in specific circumstances—such as (a), (g) and (i) above. In these cases, the command is part of the storyline. However, we then have to ask why we think that other commands of Jesus to the disciples in specific, historical contexts might apply to us—such as the instruction to take up our cross and follow him (Luke 9:23).

The command to 'take up our cross' raises another issue, namely that we may think there are some laws that apply to us but only if we understand them metaphorically (or, as in the case of cutting off our hand if it causes us to sin, as an exaggerated way of making a point). We could accept that some instructions, such as (d) above, have an indirect application to us. The tassels on clothing were intended to remind their wearers that they must obey God's laws and teachings. So, although we may not feel a compulsion to sew tassels on our trousers or dresses, we may decide to wear a dove or fish badge (the dove signifies the Holy Spirit; the fish is the ancient symbol for being a Christian), a necklace with a cross or crucifix, or a wristband with WWJD ('What Would Jesus Do?') on it, as a reminder that our primary allegiance is to God, not to ourselves or other people's preferences. Alternatively, we may feel we want to read the Bible every day and pray, to remind ourselves that we are committed to a life of obedience and service to God.

In order to help yourself to face some of the challenges of 'doing' scripture, work out in your group how you could apply the deepest meaning of the following passages. I have given some examples of people who have taken them very seriously, then some hints to provoke your imaginations.

Genesis 12:1: 'Leave your country, your relatives, and your father's home.' Think about those who have gone overseas as missionaries. Some Christians move house to live in the socially deprived areas of our cities to bring Christ's presence there. What does this verse suggest to you?

Exodus 23:14: 'Celebrate three festivals a year to honour me.' Do Christmas, Easter and Harvest count? Or is going to Spring Harvest, Easter People or Soul Survivor, or going on a week's retreat, more like it?

Mark 10:21: 'Go and sell all that you have and give the money to the poor.' Remember the life-changing influence that these words had on Francis of Assisi and, through him, the monastic movement. Think of the enormous impact of Mother Teresa—not only the practical help given to the destitute in India and around the world, but the spiritual challenge. What do these words say to us?

Luke 9:3: 'Take nothing with you for the journey.' Remember that many Celtic missionaries in the 6th century set out with this command in mind. Do we need to learn how to approach people feeling vulner-able and dependent on them—as this verse emphasizes? If so, what might that mean?

By now we should be clearer as to why we think various commands or prohibitions do or do not apply to us as Christians in the 21st century. We should also be starting to see the significance of taking scriptural commands seriously when they are appropriate to us, as well as becoming more aware that most of us have a tendency to avoid such commands when they are costly to implement at a personal level.

There is another point which is absolutely vital to grasp. In order to discern which biblical 'laws' apply to us, as well as to begin to sense how we can adapt and live them in our very different times and circumstances, we need to understand the 'big story'—the values and approaches of the Bible. As you reflect on how you tackled the four passages we have just considered, you can probably see how that bigger picture was influencing your thoughts and decisions. It is important to have the Bible in perspective and to sense what is the message of the whole of scripture. This is why a life of worship and prayer, and years of engagement with the scriptures, can and should lead us to maturity. However, it is also good to be challenged by those who are newly come to faith: they help to ensure that we are not avoiding the challenges of scripture for our own comfort, and that we have not allowed our familiarity with the Bible to tame its alien nature.

For anyone who might want to delve deeper into this huge area of biblical application, the best book I've come across is *How to Read the Bible for All It's Worth* by Gordon Fee and Douglas Stuart (SU, 2002).

DOERS OF THE WORD

Christian history and our churches today have thrown up many examples of people who have chosen to put God's word into practice, not necessarily in terms of a specific command, but more along the lines of understanding its overall direction, although sometimes this has been focused for them in a particular passage of scripture.

For instance, William Carey (1761–1834), who is regarded as the founder of the modern Protestant missions movement, sensed that God wanted a relationship with all peoples, and saw that Jesus had commissioned his disciples to take that message all round the world. At the time, Matthew 28:20 was understood to apply only to the first apostles, but Carey took it to heart for all Christians (if you like, he set it free from its original story), so eventually he went to India and began a missionary movement. Another William, William Wilberforce

(1759–1833), took seriously the Bible's view that all people were made in the image of God and therefore to be valued and respected. He recognized that slavery was incompatible with this view, even though there were many verses in the Bible that seemed to accept, if not even affirm, slavery. This led him to devote forty years to building a movement for change that led eventually to Parliament abolishing slavery.

All around our country today are individuals and groups who are seeking to apply the message of God's love for all peoples and his preference for those who, in some way or other, are disadvantaged. In my own city of Coventry, a lay person has not only started a new church, he has opened a café in an area of the city noted for its drug addiction and prostitution. The café is called 'The Gap', and is there to bridge the gap between churches and the people who live in that area, providing a place where there will be welcome, acceptance and safety. A younger person has joined his team and she is running a project called 'Roots'. She is opening up derelict council houses in the most socially deprived area of the city and enabling young Christians to settle there to become Christ's presence in that neighbourhood. Eventually they hope to be able to provide places in such houses for people who are trying to break their drug dependence or to begin a new life after prostitution.

- Think about verses and commands that would illustrate what these people did or are doing.
- Share accounts of similar stories from history or current projects that you know about. Try to discover the biblical basis for them, asking whether there are general principles or values that have shaped the person's passion or the project's aims, as well as whether there is a verse of scripture that is particularly relevant or which encapsulates the purpose.

FACING UP TO IT!

Here are some more challenging ways in which Christians are 'doing the Bible', suggesting how we can encounter the reality of the Bible by living it out.

- The Evangelical Alliance's *FaceValues* initiative for 2002 included nationwide encouragement to become involved in local social action projects which would implement some of the commands of the Bible in terms of caring for the marginalized. Find out from the Evangelical Alliance where a project has been going on near to you, and then discover how the Bible has influenced it. Perhaps you can become involved with that project, or perhaps you will be inspired to work on one of your own.
- Interview local Christian people who are in leading positions in business or charity, or even ordinary charity workers who are Christians, and seek to discover how they are engaged in 'doing' the Bible. Find out, too, how they would value support from local churches and Christians. (This might then become your opportunity to 'do it', if you decide to become involved in supporting them.) If you come up with some exciting stories, you could suggest that the local media use your research as the basis for some programmes or articles.
- Obtain a copy of *My Word* by Diana Parsk (Hodder & Stoughton 2002), a compendium of favourite passages from 200 contemporary celebrities. Discuss why you think the various people chose the passages they did, perhaps by listing what is reflected from the passage in the life and career of the celebrity. Have any of the celebrities chosen a surprising passage—one that seems to conflict with their personality? You could even write to some of the celebrities and ask them to explain why the passage is their favourite.

GO AND DO LIKEWISE

Alternatively, run a 'time/service pledge' scheme for your church or group of churches. Ask people to indicate what abilities they have and how much time (per week or per month) they could give to use that talent to serve people in the community. The offer of service could be decorating, gardening, driving a car to take people to hospital or for a 'fun run', but it could also be filling in forms, passing on skills to others, or visiting the lonely or elderly. Another team could go door to door (or operate with organizations like Age Concern) to find out what needs are in the community, and then match them with offers of help. It could also be illuminating and interesting to share the stories that emerge.

Take a biblical command or story that you sense is significant for your personal situation and see how you can start to work it through. For instance, if you have a renewed sense of concern for the environment through reading Genesis 1—2, you could become involved in an organization like Greenpeace. If this is your way of applying Genesis 1—2, then it is important that you are constantly seeking, in a creative and constructive way, to add the insights that the Bible brings—it may therefore be useful if at least two people work together so that they can support and inform one another as well as the organization concerned. Or, you could work locally to improve the environment—perhaps by organizing a litter-picking campaign or, in co-operation with the local council, bulb planting in a grassy area.

If the scriptural passage that gains your attention is to do with caring for strangers or marginalized groups, ways for you to do this would be to become involved in supporting asylum seekers, or setting up an after-schools club for children whose parents are still at work.

FURTHER AFIELD

Research people in your area who have lived out some biblical truths and the impact on the community; go to Westminster Abbey, and view the new 'Twentieth Century Martyrs' statues and find out more about their lives; or visit Cadbury World in Birmingham and try to find out about the biblical vision that inspired Quakers like William Cadbury and Joseph Rowntree to provide humane conditions for their workers, in the factory and at home.

PRAYER

Creative God, you spoke and the universe was born; you spoke again and laws were established; you spoke once more and Jesus was conceived.

All-powerful God, help us, like you, to be those who live out your words.

Lord God, show us what it is that you are asking of us and show us too how you are there with us to make this possible. Amen.

Chapter 9

GIVE IT AWAY

ICE-BREAKERS

1. Ask everyone to bring a wrapped present (costing not more than £1) to the meeting. (Alternatively, ask them to bring an 'unwanted' Christmas or birthday gift, wrapped, of course, and disguised if necessary.) Place the presents in a black sack and invite each person to pick out a present. They are then invited to explain what they think of their surprise gift!
2. Free gifts are never really free. What's your experience?
3. Pair up with someone you know. Then imagine (a) what you would like as a present, and (b) what you think your partner would like, if £2 was the limit. Write your presents down and then share your choices. How near did you get to guessing each other's wishes?
4. The group has been given £1 million to give away. Work out how you would disperse this wealth.

INTRODUCTION

Over the last 200 years and more, organizations like Bible Society, Scripture Gift Mission, Open Doors and many more have given away millions of portions of scriptures, as well as New Testaments and complete Bibles. This has been driven by the understanding that the Bible is a very special book. People have been prepared to die to ensure that it could be translated into the common languages of people around the world, and to ensure its distribution in frequently dangerous physical environments and hostile political situations. This task of making the scriptures available continues, and a vital part of the chain are ordinary people who, in a variety of ways, seek to give the Bible (or parts of it) away. Sometimes this is done directly, through face-to-face gifts; at other times it is done through people's financial gifts, making it possible for others thousands of miles away to receive Bibles they could not afford themselves. This chapter looks at some issues which encourage us to give the Bible away and then some creative ways to do this in our context. Our first step is to look at some passages from the Bible itself which provide insight into this task and privilege.

BIBLE STUDY

We begin by taking a look at the parable of the sower, which can be found in Matthew 13:1–9, Mark 4:1–9, and Luke 8:4–8. As with so many of Jesus' parables, this story relates an incident taken from everyday life. It tells of a man sowing seed—but his method was different from the way we plant seeds in our garden or how farmers sow crops today, with all their complicated equipment. The normal practice in Jesus' day was to take handfuls of seed and throw it in drifts towards the ground, as we might sprinkle grass seed on our lawn. The parable goes on to tell what happened to the seed. But why did Jesus use such stories?

Preachers who use stories in their sermons to make their points clearer have frequently thought that this was why Jesus used them, too. However, this does not quite correspond to Jesus' reply when the disciples asked him why he spoke in stories to the crowds. Listen to what he says: 'The reason I use parables in talking to them is that they look, but do not see, and they listen, but do not hear or understand' (Matthew 13:13).

Scholars today are less confident that Jesus told homely stories so that people could easily grasp the nature of his message. Rather, the view now is that he used stories, in contrast to more straightforward didactic teaching, because stories embed themselves in our minds. Further, because they do not necessarily have a simple resolution, they can help to prise open closed views and therefore give people the opportunity to look at things differently. To put the same thing in other words, the parables create the potential for seeing the world, God and ourselves in a different kind of way. They help to free us up to receive new truth—the truth of God's Kingdom. The parable of the sower is recognized in the Gospels as crucial for understanding how God's truth operates in our lives, which is why I have raised the question about parables in general here. This parable is about grasping God's message.

For many years the logo used by Bible Society was taken from a London statue of 'The Sower', who is clearly the main character, although not the focus, for this parable. New times demand new logos, however, and Bible Society discovered that fewer and fewer people knew the story that the 'sower' figure represented, so they changed their logo to a more abstract star-shaped image. But the parable to which this image relates is still foundational for our attitudes to the Bible, as a prime source of the 'word of God'. At the heart of this story, as we shall see, is the challenge to 'give it away'.

As Jesus' explanation about the purpose of parables indicates, any attempt to bypass the story itself is likely to mean that it fails in its task of probing open our fixed perspectives. It is important that we listen to his words before seeking to say, 'This is what it means'! So here it is:

Now listen! A farmer went out to scatter seed in a field. While the farmer was scattering the seed, some of it fell along the road and was eaten by birds. Other seeds fell on thin, rocky ground and quickly started growing because the soil wasn't very deep. But when the sun came up, the plants were scorched and dried up, because they did not have enough roots. Some other seeds fell where thorn bushes grew up and choked out the plants. So they did not produce any

grain. But a few seeds did fall on good ground where the plants grew and produced thirty or sixty or even a hundred times as much as was scattered.
MARK 4:3–8 (CEV)

Some of the points to note are:

- The fruitfulness of the seed depends on the receptivity of the soil but also on prevailing conditions.
- Results from sowing are not instantly apparent: it takes time for the seed to germinate, let alone produce a crop.
- While the results are very varied, the overall outcome is secure and justifies the risk.
- Jesus calls us to guard what is sown in our lives while being liberal in the way we distribute it to others.

For those who first heard this story, every time they saw a sower at work, there was the possibility that they would remember the story of Jesus and be challenged again. One of the ways in which it provokes us all is to ask the question, 'Why, if so much of the seed was wasted (after all, three parts of the story are about the seed being lost and only one about producing a harvest), why would the farmer bother?' Obviously, the answer is that the harvest outweighed the wastage. Careful research has shown us that Jesus was emphasizing this point. In Palestine at that time, a thirtyfold increase would have been considered a phenomenal harvest. So Jesus was shocking his hearers (although we cannot always see it, there is usually a shock element in each story he tells!) by assuring them that God's message would be exceptionally productive, even though it may not look promising to start with. This challenges us today: if we want any kind of spiritual harvest we must take the risk and sow God's word, even in unlikely places, and do it enthusiastically, believing that the world is structured by God to ensure a great harvest—in the end.

Equally, we should not be too disappointed, and certainly not give up, if we do not always get results. It is not the fault of the seed or the sower.

This parable of Jesus is not the only place where God's message is related to the growth of seed. Here are three such Bible passages which express ways in which God's word operates: 1 Corinthians 3:5–9; John 4:35–38; Isaiah 55:11. Take a look at these passages, noting what they suggest about God's word in terms of its nature, effectiveness and distribution. Together they are a stimulus to us to become involved in spreading the message. We can gain still more impetus by learning how important the Bible can be in changing people's lives for the better. From the hundreds of stories available, here are just a couple.

A LOOK AT THE HARVEST

Antonio, of São Paulo in Brazil, had a violent alcoholic father, struggled with asthma and turned to drugs. He was stabbed in a gang fight. Recovering in hospital, he was given a New Testament, which he started to read. This prompted him to forgive the person who had stabbed him, and started his journey to faith. He is now pastor of a church. He writes, 'I praise and thank God for the Bible Society of Brazil because it was through the Bibles and leaflets that they distributed that I had this great encounter with God' (*Word in Action*, Spring 2001, page 6).

In parts of Russia and Africa, the Bible, especially the New Testament, is provided on audio cassette for people who cannot read at all or only with considerable difficulty, or who cannot read the Bible because it has not been translated into their language. Normally a group of people will gather round a cassette player and listen to the Bible reading together. There is normally much excitement and a great impact made as God's word appears to address them very directly, in their own spoken language.

Since 1999 the Azeri New Testament has been available on cassette. This is a description of how it is being used in Azerbaijan.

Most listening sessions are held in people's homes or other informal environments, according to distributors who have travelled thousands of kilometres to let Azeri speakers hear the word of God in their own language.

Mikhail is one such distributor who has seen lives changed through the programme. During one trip to a small village on the southern slopes of the Caucasus mountains, he organized a listening session in the home of a family so poor that their house did not even have a door. Poverty had left them without hope.

One man in the group was there under protest—he did not believe the stories that Mikhail had told about Jesus, and said he was not interested in hearing any more. But as the tape began to play, he fell silent. When he heard the same stories about Jesus that Mikhail had told he was amazed.

'Are these words from the real Holy Book?' he asked. 'I thought you had just made them up.'

After two more hours of listening, he stood up, embraced Mikhail and said that he had been changed by what he had heard.

Mikhail was to receive more good news when he returned to that home a few months later. The poor family thanked him because their apple orchard had yielded an excellent harvest and hope had returned to them. Others from the village also stopped Mikhail to tell him how hearing God's word had brought joy to their lives.

UNITED BIBLE SOCIETIES WORLD REPORT 358, MARCH 2001, PAGE 7.

So, whatever the format, the Bible can have an enriching and even life-changing impact on people. But often someone needs to make it available as a gift because people either cannot afford it or will not bother to obtain it.

It is time now for us to look at some ways in which we can become involved in this challenging but rewarding task of 'giving it away'.

HOW TO GIVE IT AWAY

SPECIAL OCCASIONS

Infant baptisms and dedication services, as well as weddings, have traditionally been special occasions for giving Bibles, and there are special editions published for these events. There are valid reasons for marking these life-transitions with a Bible. For one thing, they emphasize that the Bible is a fundamental guide for finding our way through life. However, the down-side to this tradition is that normally the translation given is the Authorized Version, which most people today, especially if they do not have a church background, find difficult to understand. The unfortunate implication can be that as the language is out of date, so the message will be irrelevant to people in the 21st century. Also, if the Bible is presented to a baby being welcomed into the family of the Church, the child will be unable to read the Bible for themselves, or even absorb very much if it is read to them, for many years. By then the Bible may well have been lost. Inadvertently, instead of acting as an indispensable guide to life, it can appear as a relic from the past. When it comes to weddings, the situation is probably worse. A Bible may be presented along with silver horseshoes and so can appear like a superficial lucky charm rather than the key to the mystery of the universe.

Find out how the above comments correspond to the experiences of people in your group.

- As a group, discuss what Bibles you have received as gifts on special occasions and what you (a) feel or felt about them, and (b) did or do with them.
- You may also wish to ask friends and colleagues who are not openly Christians the same questions and compare the findings.
- If you have friends who belong to other faiths, you may want to find out how they regard their holy books, when they are likely to receive or give them as presents and how they regard such gifts.

Of course, God is sovereign and no doubt there are powerful stories about how he has used such gift Bibles, but there may be better ways to use special occasions.

Brainstorm within your group, bearing in mind the insights you have gleaned from the earlier questions and your own ideas for 'giving it away' at special moments in people's lives. Here are a few ideas:

- Give a children's Bible (or Bible stories) to a child who is starting school.
- Give a 'Youth Bible' when they move on to secondary school.
- Might a Bible portion be appropriate when people move to university or start work?
- Rather than a Bible for the baby at baptism, what about a contemporary version for the parents when they have their first baby?
- Whenever you choose to give away a Bible, how about including a letter or card, explaining why you are giving the Bible and pointing out some relevant stories or verses?

Don't forget to include, in your brainstorming, Bible formats other than printed ones—although these can sometimes be more expensive than print. For instance, why not give an electronic Bible to someone to mark their entry into teenage years (or somebody reaching double figures). For a child starting school, you could provide a video based on the Bible (*Testament*, *Storykeepers* or *The Miracle Maker*). Or, if you are a grandparent with regular contact with your grandchildren, buy copies of these videos for the times when they come to visit you, and watch them together. Why not provide some part of the Bible on cassette for someone who has just passed their driving test, or obtain a foreign-language version for someone who has passed a GCSE in the subject?

There are three principles being applied in the above suggestions which you can bear in mind as you come up with your own ideas.

- Pick occasions which are significant for the person involved.
- Find the right format for the right occasion.
- Look for a context which will encourage use rather than storage.

HELPING OTHERS TO GIVE IT AWAY

Organizations like the Gideons or Christians in Sport specialize in giving away the Bible (or parts of it, especially the New Testament). Whereas the Gideons work in a steady, ongoing process, seeking to place Bibles in hotels, hospitals and prisons, together with their extensive schools distribution project, Christians in Sport focus on special opportunities, such as the Commonwealth and Olympic Games. One way to give the Bible away is to become involved in prayer, finance or even, where appropriate, working with such groups as a volunteer. With the Gideons in particular, you may be able to focus your efforts locally. Full Gideon membership is open to men only, on recommendation by your minister and the local branch, but wives of Gideons work closely alongside their husbands in most areas of the work as well as having special responsibility for the medical profession. However, both men and women can become 'Friends' and contribute to the work in a variety of ways. To contact either the Gideons or Christians in Sport to find out how you can help, please see the Resources section.

SEND IT FAR AWAY

One of the messages of the parable of the sower is that some soil is more fertile than others. We do know that, as well as special times, there are special places in the world where the Bible is needed desperately. These places are much more likely to produce a 'high-yield harvest'. We will probably not know who received our gift, but Jesus assures us that what we do 'in secret' is noticed by our Father in heaven and one day we will receive the acknowledgment that our action deserves (Matthew 6:6, 18). So here are a few practical ideas.

Bible Society runs an imaginative scheme called 'Bible a Month Club'. The idea is simple but with a twist. As with any book club, people are asked to pay for reduced-price books, with a subscription from £3 a month upwards. As with a normal club, people receive information about the products. So what is the twist? Subscribers do not get the benefit themselves. Rather, someone in a part of the world where scripture is scarce will receive a copy of the Bible that they can understand. For instance, disabled children living in Tanzania have benefited. In this case the gift of a Bible was linked to a reading and writing project, which brought a new sense of self-worth to these children. Similarly, in the mountains of Peru where many adult people cannot read, they have been supplied with dramatized readings of the New Testament on audio cassette.

Although the subscribing members do not receive the books, they do get some benefits! They are sent prayer cards featuring information about the countries and projects being supported, maps and prayer topics. But, of course, the greatest benefit is knowing that they are making God's word available to people who would otherwise not know about it. Over one billion people cannot afford a Bible, another billion people have yet to hear the gospel and a further one billion will be added to the world's population by 2013.

USING YOUR CREATIVITY

One way to 'add value' to a gift of part or all of the Bible is by giving our time to create an attractive presentation of it, using craft gifts that we may have. In this age when time is everything, we can help people to sense that we value them and the Bible by designing and producing our own scripture-related gift objects. In some cases, the type of gift may mean that it is shown to others or even put on permanent display in the home.

For practical ideas, have another look at Chapter 4, 'Display It'.

For many people today, the computer is a more familiar tool than the sewing machine or paintbrush. This too provides us with opportunities. You could, for instance, design your own e-cards to send to friends.

If these gifts are made at a evening class or club, another dimension is that those you spend time with will see what you are doing and you will have the opportunity to explain why the Bible matters.

FURTHER AFIELD

Why not plan an evening when your group (perhaps with invited guests) can find out about the importance of the Bible in other parts of the world, and so both be motivated to 'give it away' and also discover an effective channel for doing it? One way would be to invite a speaker from one of the Bible-related organizations listed in the Resources section. To make the event rather more exciting, you could also design the evening as a 'tour' of the country that you are learning about. Have 'boarding passes' for gaining entry, and arrange the seats aeroplane-style. You may be able to obtain pictures and posters from a travel agent or that country's tourist board, and all kinds of information from relevant websites. Once 'passengers' are on board, explain about take-off and what will take place during the evening, and play music from that country. You could even display a map of the country and explain the geography. Either while they are 'travelling' or halfway through the presentation, serve food which has associations with the country.

Or plan a Mystery Tour using Bible verses as clues—perhaps making a small charge so that the money could be donated. A Mystery Tour involves following a trail of clues such as 'Drive to village x, locate the red telephone kiosk and there you will find the next clue.' A biblical clue might say, 'Take the colour of sin (Isaiah 1:18) and add to Jeremiah 33:3 (AV). There you will find your next move.' Of course, the clues can be less cryptic! You could use references to 'Bethel' to identify a chapel with that name, or 'Mary' for a parish church of St Mary. For a recreation ground, you might use references to children playing. Pub names such as 'The Sycamore Tree', 'The Bull's Head' or 'The Cross Keys' might suggest Bible verses, and many other notable features, such as war memorials, graveyards, rivers and crossroads can be indicated by biblical references. All it requires is a little imagination and ingenuity.

Eventually, the trail of clues (either hidden at the location or placed in easily recognized A4 envelopes) should lead people back to the starting point (in which case they need to keep a record of the places they have visited), or to another venue where refreshments are provided. It is probably advisable for each team to have a mobile phone and for someone to be contactable to give help to those who get lost.

PRAYER

Lord God, the better we know the Bible, the better we know what you are like. The clearer we see what you are like, the clearer we see how generous you are. The more we experience your generosity, the more we want to be generous too.

Father, as we have come to appreciate the Bible more, the more we long to throw open its doors for others to look in and be surprised, and to walk in and to be at home. We commit ourselves to the task of making the Bible available in ways that will attract others to it and help them overcome their prejudices against it. Please show us who you want us to serve in this way and give us your generosity to help us fulfil this commitment to you. Amen.

CONCLUSION

Whether you have worked through the whole book on your own or tackled it as a group, you will have learnt to approach the Bible in a number of ways. Each of them requires that you interact with the text of scripture, often using not only your mind but other facilities that God has given you. We have approached the Bible this way deliberately, on the understanding that there are levels of meaning and significance which can best be obtained by more than straightforward reading and study, and which will nourish us for living today. I do hope you have discovered that this is true for you and that you now realize you can supplement your normal Bible diet, whether that comes to you through mainly liturgical, expository or devotional approaches.

In conclusion, I want to encourage you to keep your eyes open for all the new ways of encountering the Bible that continue to emerge. Not only because there will be many new resources from the electronics and media worlds, but because there are already other ways of gaining greatly from the Bible. All of these will help us to go on interacting with the most amazing story ever told, which can be retold in a thousand ways.

In the end, of course, what really matters is not the method but the miracle of a God who made us, in Christ, loved and forgave us and who now longs for a fulfilling relationship with us. But if the ideas in this book and others that you come across can help you and others to discover or rediscover the fascinating joy and truth of God's story, then our time has been more than well spent.

To many, the Bible may seem hard, cold and uninteresting—like the frosted packages in the deep freeze, but with a little patience and ingenuity all sorts of nutritious and fascinating meals can be served up. This, at least, is my experience with this sacred text. I hope it is yours and that you can use this book to serve up appetizing 'meals' for others, so that they in turn become creative Bible cooks!

RESOURCES

USEFUL CONTACT DETAILS

BIBLE SOCIETIES

(In England and Wales) Bible Society, Stonehill Green, Westlea, Swindon SN7 5DG
Scottish Bible Society, 7 Hampton Terrace, Edinburgh EH12 5XU
Bible Society in Northern Ireland, 27 Howard Street, Belfast BT1 6NN
United Bible Society, World Service Centre, 12 Bridge House, 7th Floor, Reading RG1 8PJ

OTHER BIBLE AGENCIES

Christians in Sport, PO Box 93, Oxford OX2 7YP
Open Doors, PO Box 6, Witney, Oxon OX8 7SP
The Gideons International (British Isles), Western House, George Street, Lutterworth LE17 4EE
Scripture Gift Mission (International office and Britain), 3 Eccleston Street, London SW1W 9LZ
Wycliffe Bible Translators, Horsleys Green, High Wycombe, Bucks HP14 3XL. (Offices also at 19 Beechill Park South, Belfast, BT8 4PB and 2 Oxgangs Path, Edinburgh EH13 9LX)

BIBLE NOTES PUBLISHERS

Bible Alive, 124 City Road, Stoke-on-Trent ST4 2PH
BRF, First Floor, Elsfield House, 15–17 Elsfield Way, Oxford OX2 8FG
Crusade for World Reveival, PO Box 230, Farnham, Surrey GU9 8XG
IBRA, 1020 Bristol Road, Selly Oak, Birmingham B29 6LB

Scripture Union, 207–209 Queensway, Bletchley, Milton Keynes MK2 2EB (also at 9 Canal Street, Glasgow G4 0AB)

LITERATURE

INTRODUCTION

Let There Be Light by David Daniell (The British Library, 1994) gives a brief, illustrated history of Tyndale's life.

PLAY IT

A useful resource for children (11–14 especially) is provided by *Absolutely Everything* by Terry Clutterham, published by CPAS and Scripture Union, which is designed to give an overview of the story and themes of the Bible. Each session is based around a team action game. Terry's philosophy is, 'Games can provide the mix of skills, attitudes and knowledge that is vital for memorable learning to take place.'

A good basic book for all kinds of dramatizations is Michael Perry (ed.), *The Dramatised Bible* (Marshall Pickering, 1988). This sets out large parts of the Bible for dramatic reading.

REWRITE IT

Door Posts by Timothy Botts (Tyndale House Publishers, 1986) gives much insight into calligraphy as a creative art form, as well as interesting and varied illustrations.

If you want to organize a workshop on Calligraphy and the Bible, then contact Derek Harley, 45 Newcastle Road, Leek, ST13 5RT; e-mail d.a.harley@talk21.com

EAT IT

For materials on the Passover/*Seder* contact The Church's Ministry

Among the Jews, Audio Visual Department, 30c Clarence Road, St Albans, Herts AL1 4JJ.

For an idea on how to give a shared meal special meaning, Jenny Baker's *Jesus at the Centre* (Paternoster, 2001, pp. 12–15) is good.

TWIST IT

The Telling Place (Hetton Hall, Chatton, Alnwick, Northumberland NE66 5SD; 01289 388477; e-mail thetellingplace@bigfoot.com) is based at a Christian community and has been exploring the potential of storytelling with Bible Society. They run training courses both at Hetton Hall and for churches in their own locations. They have developed an extensive network of storytellers and are running an apprenticeship scheme. A bulletin, giving details of developments, is available.

PRAY IT

Two books are particularly illuminating for appreciating the prayers of the Bible.

The first is by R.E. Clements, who unpacks many Old Testament and some New Testament prayers in *Prayers of the Bible* (SCM Press, 1985). He provides a rich account of the historical background and concludes with a reflection on the significance of the prayer.

The second forms a kind of companion, *The Prayers of the New Testament* by Donald Coggan (Hodder and Stoughton, 1967). It lists around 100 separate prayers (not including Revelation 22:17 or Luke 1:46–55!). Each prayer receives a helpful commentary but there are also some valuable introductions, which take in some of the direct teaching we have on prayer as well as unpacking the significance of the way Jesus and Paul, for instance, actually prayed.

Unfortunately neither book is easily available—although it is always worth checking with your bookshop to see if they have been reprinted. You could also try looking in second-hand bookshops or asking your minister.

My own book, *Dangerous Praying* (Scripture Union, 2000), looks at the prayers in Ephesians and how they can enrich our prayer life today.

If you cannot get hold of these books, then looking up words like 'pray' and 'prayer' in a concordance or, better still, a topical concordance will lead you to most of the prayers in the Bible.

In addition to recorded prayers, we should not forget that the book of Psalms is essentially a prayer book. One way to explore it is through Eugene Peterson's *Answering God—Learning to Pray from the Psalms* (Marshall Pickering, 1989). He explores how the psalms are not pious platitudes but people exploring and expressing the pain as well as the joy of life. He also emphasizes that prayer is always our response to God, even when we think we are initiating the conversation.

A different approach to using the Psalms for developing a prayer life is *You Shall Not Want: A Spiritual Journey Based on the Psalms* by Richard Chilson (Ave Maria Press, 1996).

For a basic introduction to *Lectio Divina*, see Michael de Verteuil, *Your Word is a Light for my Steps* (Veritas, 1998).

STUDY IT

The Christian Resources Exhibition, which is held at Sandown each May and in one of the major cities of the UK each autumn, provides a marvellous opportunity to discover the latest material available for Bible study, whether books, audio, video or CD-ROM. Several hundred Christian organizations are there displaying their products and there is also a lecture programme.

For a basic commentary series, a good place to start is *The People's Bible Commentary* (BRF) or *Crossway Bible Guides*, or *Tyndale Old and New Testament Commentaries* (IVP).

DO IT

Tony Dobson's *Ready Made Assemblies* (Scripture Union, 2000) is an excellent introduction to more than 24 significant Christians who have lived out the biblical vision. Many are historical figures such as Josiah

Speers, John Newton and William Carey, but others are contemporary sportspeople and people who have been in the news, like Gordon Wilson and Terry Waite. Although prepared for use in school assemblies, there is enough information and stimulation to be helpful for our purposes too.

A more detailed look at some similar kinds of people is *Signs of Contradiction* by David Alton (Hodder and Stoughton 1996).

The Evangelical Alliance's address is:
Whitefield House
186 Kennington Park Road
London
SE11 4BT
Tel: 020 7207 2100
E-mail info@eauk.org

GIVE IT AWAY

Scripture Gift Mission provide attractively packaged scripture portions, and a display-stand for church use. They supply materials for all ages, though mostly for adults. Scripture portions are free of charge, but donations are invited.

Open Doors has for many years provided scriptures for communist countries. Their ministry was made famous by their adventurous and courageous founder, Brother Andrew. They continue to work in countries closed to the gospel, including those dominated by Islam.

Wycliffe Bible Translators are one of the key organizations involved in translating the Bible into new languages.

NOTES

1. In a letter from Margaret Barratt to the author, 11 January 2000.
2. E.H.C. Corathiel, *Oberammergau and its Passion Play*, (Burns & Oates, 1950), p 37.
3. Corathiel, p. 39.
4. For these and more examples, see M.H. Manser, *The Amazing Book of Bible Facts* (Marshall Pickering, 1990).
5. The Good News Bible's preferred translation here is 'power', not 'spirit' or 'Spirit', for *ruach*. (*Ruach* is the Hebrew word which can be translated 'wind' or 'Spirit': which one is correct depends on the context.) In view of the emphasis on the divine origin of all this craftsman's skills here, it is strange not to use the normal translation of 'Spirit'—hence my substitution.
6. J.B. Taylor, *Ezekiel* (IVP, 1976), p. 64.
7. Many people find it helpful to start Bible meditation in the context of a retreat. The Retreat Association's publications are very helpful. Their contact details are 258 Bermondsey Street, London SE1 3UJ; e-mail info@retreats.org.uk
8. For a brief introduction and some further references, see Richard Foster, *Prayer* (Hodder and Stoughton, 1992), pp. 62–63.
9. The Revd Dr Seamus O'Connell—unpublished paper on *Lectio Divina*, page 4.
10. One of the richest memories I have of praying the Lord's Prayer was when I was leading a group on a tour of Israel. On the Mount of Olives is the Eleona Basilica, the home of Carmelite nuns. The covered walkways around the courtyard contain ceramic plaques which have the Lord's Prayer in over 80 languages. Although my group could manage only six languages between us, we prayed in them. It created a wonderful sense of the universality of the impact of the gospel, as we prayed these words 'each in our own tongue'.
11. *A Bunch of Everlastings or Texts That Made History* (Epworth Press, 1920). As far as I know, the book is no longer in print, but may be available second-hand or from a local library.

ANSWERS TO 'LIVING BY THE WORD' EXERCISE

A	Sir Walter Scott	John 9:4
B	Martin Luther	Romans 1:17
C	Sir John Franklin	Isaiah 43:2
D	John Bunyan	John 6:37
E	John Wesley	Mark 12:34
F	William Cowper	Romans 3:24
G	William Carey	Isaiah 54:2
H	William Wilberforce	Luke 18:13